Euripedes and His Age by Gilbert Murray

Euripides is rightly lauded as one of the great dramatists of all time. In his lifetime, he wrote over 90 plays and although only 18 have survived they reveal the scope and reach of his genius. In this volume the excellent translator Gilbert Murray explores the life, plays and society of Euripides to bring us a greater and more nuanced understanding of the great man himself.

Euripides is identified with many theatrical innovations that have influenced drama all the way down to modern times, especially in the representation of traditional, mythical heroes as ordinary people in extraordinary circumstances.

As would be expected from a life lived 2,500 years ago, details of it are few and far between. Accounts of his life, written down the ages, do exist but whether much is reliable or surmised is open to debate.

Most accounts agree that he was born on Salamis Island around 480 BC, to mother Cleito and father Mnesarchus, a retailer who lived in a village near Athens. Upon the receipt of an oracle saying that his son was fated to win "crowns of victory", Mnesarchus insisted that the boy should train for a career in athletics.

However, what is clear is that athletics was not to be the way to win crowns of victory. Euripides had been lucky enough to have been born in the era as the other two masters of Greek Tragedy; Sophocles and Æschylus. It was in their footsteps that he was destined to follow.

His first play was performed some thirteen years after the first of Socrates plays and a mere three years after Æschylus had written his classic The Oristria.

Theatre was becoming a very important part of the Greek culture. The Dionysia, held annually, was the most important festival of theatre and second only to the fore-runner of the Olympic games, the Panathenia, held every four years, in appeal.

Euripides first competed in the City Dionysia, in 455 BC, one year after the death of Æschylus, and, incredibly, it was not until 441 BC that he won first prize. His final competition in Athens was in 408 BC. The Bacchae and Iphigenia in Aulis were performed after his death in 405 BC and first prize was awarded posthumously. Altogether his plays won first prize only five times.

Euripides was also a great lyric poet. In Medea, for example, he composed for his city, Athens, "the noblest of her songs of praise". His lyric skills however are not just confined to individual poems: "A play of Euripides is a musical whole....one song echoes motifs from the preceding song, while introducing new ones."

Much of his life and his whole career coincided with the struggle between Athens and Sparta for hegemony in Greece but he didn't live to see the final defeat of his city.

Euripides fell out of favour with his fellow Athenian citizens and retired to the court of Archelaus, king of Macedon, who treated him with consideration and affection.

At his death, in around 406BC, he was mourned by the king, who, refusing the request of the Athenians that his remains be carried back to the Greek city, buried him with much splendor within his own dominions. His tomb was placed at the confluence of two streams, near Arethusa in Macedonia, and a cenotaph was built to his memory on the road from Athens towards the Piraeus.

Index of Contents

EURIPIDES AND HIS AGE

CHAPTER I

INTRODUCTORY

Most of the volumes of this series are occupied with large subjects and subjects commonly recognized as important to great masses of people at the present day. In devoting the present volume to the study of a single writer, remote from us in time and civilization and scarcely known by more than name to many readers of the Library, I am moved by the belief that, quite apart from his disputed greatness as a poet and thinker, apart from his amazing and perhaps unparalleled success as a practical playwright, Euripides is a figure of high significance in the history of humanity and of special interest to our own generation.

Born, according to the legend, in exile and fated to die in exile, Euripides, in whatever light one regards him, is a man of curious and ironic history. As a poet he has lived through the ages in an atmosphere of controversy, generally—though by no means always—loved by poets and despised by critics. As a thinker he is even to this day treated almost as a personal enemy by scholars of orthodox and conformist minds; defended, idealized and sometimes transformed beyond recognition by various champions of rebellion and the free intellect. The greatest difficulty that I feel in writing about him is to keep in mind without loss of proportion anything like the whole activity of the many-sided man. Recent writers have tended to emphasize chiefly his work as a destructive thinker. Dr. Verrall, the most brilliant of all modern critics of Euripides, to whose pioneer work my own debt is greater than I can well express, entitled one of his books "Euripides the Rationalist" and followed to its extreme limit the path indicated by this particular clue. His vivid and interesting disciple Professor Norwood has followed him. In Germany Dr. Nestlé, in a sober and learned book, treating of Euripides as a thinker, says that "all mysticism was fundamentally repugnant to him"; a view which is certainly wrong, since some of the finest expressions of Greek mysticism known to us are taken from the works of Euripides. Another good writer, Steiger, draws an elaborate parallel between Euripides and Ibsen and finds the one key to Euripides in his realism and his absolute devotion to truth. Yet an older generation of Euripides-lovers felt these things quite differently. When Macaulay proclaimed that there was absolutely nothing in literature to equal The Bacchae, he was certainly not thinking about rationalism or realism. He felt the romance, the magic, the sheer poetry. So did Milton and Shelley and Browning. And so did the older English scholars like Porson and Elmsley. Porson, while admitting that the critics have many things to say against Euripides as compared, for instance, with Sophocles, answers in his inarticulate way "illum admiramur, hunc legimus"—"we admire the one, but we read the other." Elmsley, so far from regarding Euripides as mainly a thinker, remarks in passing that he was a poet singularly addicted to contradicting himself. To Porson and Elmsley the poetry of Euripides might or might not be good on the highest plane, it was at any rate delightful. Quite different again are the momentous judgments pronounced upon him as a writer of tragedy by two of the greatest judges. Aristotle, writing at a period when Euripides was rather out of fashion, and subjecting him to much serious and sometimes unintelligent criticism, considers him still "the most tragic of the poets." And Goethe, after expressing his surprise at the general belittling of Euripides by "the aristocracy of philologists, led by the buffoon Aristophanes," asks emphatically: "Have all the nations of the world since his time produced one dramatist who was worthy to hand him his slippers?" (Tagebüchern, November 22, 1831.) We must try, if we can, to bear duly in mind all these different lines of approach.

As a playwright the fate of Euripides has been strange. All through a long life he was almost invariably beaten in the State competitions. He was steadily admired by some few philosophers, like Socrates; he enjoyed immense fame throughout Greece; but the official judges of poetry were against him, and his own people of Athens admired him reluctantly and with a grudge.

After death, indeed, he seemed to come into his kingdom. He held the stage as no other tragedian has ever held it, and we hear of his plays being performed with popular success six hundred years after they were written, and in countries far removed from Greece. He influenced all the higher forms of Greek writing, both in prose and poetry. He is more quoted by subsequent writers than any other Greek tragedian; nay, if we leave out of count mere dictionary references to rare words, he is more quoted than all the other tragedians together. And nineteen of his plays have survived to our own day as against seven each of Aeschylus and Sophocles. This seems enough glory for any man. Yet the fate that grudged him prizes in his lifetime contrived afterwards to spread a veneer of commonplaceness over the success which it could not prevent. To a great extent Euripides was read because he was, or seemed, easy; the older poets were neglected because they were difficult. Attic Greek in his hands had begun to assume the form in which it remained for a thousand years as the recognized literary language of the east of Europe and the great instrument and symbol of civilization. He was a treasure-house of Attic style and ancient maxims, and eminently useful to orators who liked quotations. Meantime the melody and meaning of his lyrics were lost, because men had forgotten the pronunciation of fifth-century Greek and could no longer read lyrics intelligently. The obviously exciting quality of his plays kept its effect; but there was no one to understand the subtlety of his craftsmanship, the intimate study of character, the skilful forging of links and clashes between scenes, the mastery of that most wonderful of Greek dramatic instruments, the Chorus. Plays had practically ceased to be written. They were thought of either as rhetorical exercises or as spectacles for the amphitheatre. Something similar happened to the whole inward spirit in which he worked, call it philosophy or call it religion. Its meaning became obscured. It had indeed a powerful influence on the philosophers of the great fourth century schools: they probably understood at least one side of him. But the sayings of his that are quoted broadcast and repeated through author after author of the decadence are mostly thoughts of quite the second rank, which have lost half their value by being torn from their context, often commonplace, often—as is natural in fragments of dramas—mutually contradictory, though almost always simply and clearly expressed.

It was this clear expression which the late Greeks valued so highly. "Clarity"—saphêneia—was the watchword of style in Euripides' own day and remained always the foremost aim of Greek rhetoric. Indeed what a Greek called "rhetorikê" often implied the very opposite of what we call "rhetoric." To think clearly, to arrange your matter under formal heads, to have each paragraph definitely articulated and each sentence simply and exactly expressed: that was the main lesson of the Greek rhetor. The tendency was already beginning in classical times and no classical writer carried it further than Euripides. But here again Fate has been ironical with him. The ages that were incapable of understanding him loved him for his clearness: our own age, which might at last understand him, is instinctively repelled by it. We do not much like a poet to be very clear, and we hate him to be formal. We are clever readers, quick in the up-take, apt to feel flattered and stimulated by a little obscurity; mystical philosophy is all very well in a poet, but clear-cut intellect—no. At any rate we are sharply offended by "firstlys, secondlys and thirdlys," by divisions on the one hand and on the other hand. And all this and more Euripides insists on giving us.

It is the great obstacle between him and us. Apart from it we have only to exercise a little historical imagination and we shall find in him a man, not indeed modern—half his charm is that he is so remote and austere—but a man who has in his mind the same problems as ourselves, the same doubts and largely the same ideals; who has felt the same desires and indignations as a great number of people at the present day, especially young people. Not because young people are cleverer than old, nor yet because they are less wise; but because the poet or philosopher or martyr who lives, half-articulate, inside most human beings is apt to be smothered or starved to death in the course of middle life. As long as he is still alive we have, most of us, the key to understanding Euripides.

What, then, shall be our method in approaching him? It is fatal to fly straight at him with modern ready-made analogies. We must see him in his own atmosphere. Every man who possesses real vitality can be seen as the resultant of two forces. He is first the child of a particular age, society, convention; of what we may call in one word a tradition. He is secondly, in one degree or another, a rebel against that tradition. And the best traditions make the best rebels. Euripides is the child of a strong and splendid tradition and is, together with Plato, the fiercest of all rebels against it.

There is nothing paradoxical in this. No tradition is perfect. The best brings only a passing period of peace or triumph or stable equilibrium; humanity rests for a moment, but knows that it must travel further; to rest for ever would be to die. The most thorough conformists are probably at their best when forced to fight for their ideal against forces that would destroy it. And a tradition itself is generally at its best, not when it is universally accepted, but when it is being attacked and broken. It is then that it learns to search its own heart and live up to its full meaning. And in a sense the greatest triumph that any tradition can accomplish is to rear noble and worthy rebels. The Greek tradition of the fifth century B.C., the great age of Athens, not only achieved extraordinary advances in most departments of human life, but it trained an extraordinary band of critical or rebellious children. Many a reader of Plato's most splendid satires against democratic Athens will feel within him the conclusive answer: "No place but Athens could ever have reared such a man as this, and taught him to see these faults or conceive these ideals."

We are in reaction now against another great age, an age whose achievements in art are memorable, in literature massive and splendid, in science and invention absolutely unparalleled, but greatest of all perhaps in the raising of all standards of public duty, the humanizing of law and society, and the awakening of high ideals in social and international politics. The Victorian Age had, amid enormous differences, a certain similarity with the Periclean in its lack of self-examination, its rush and chivalry and optimism, its unconscious hypocrisy, its failure to think out its problems to the bitter end. And in most of the current criticism on things Victorian, so far as it is not mere fashion or folly, one seems to feel the Victorian spirit itself speaking. It arraigns Victorian things by a Victorian standard; blames them not because they have moved in a particular direction, but because they have not moved far enough; because so many of the things they attempted are still left undone, because the ideals they preached and the standards by which they claimed to be acting were so much harder of satisfaction than they knew. Euripides, like ourselves, comes in an age of criticism following upon an age of movement and action. And for the most part, like ourselves, he accepts the general standards on which the movement and action were based. He accepts the Athenian ideals of free thought, free speech, democracy, "virtue" and patriotism. He arraigns his country because she is false to them.

We have spoken of the tradition as a homogeneous thing, but for any poet or artist there are two quite different webs in it. There are the accepted conventions of his art and the accepted beliefs of his intellect, the one set aiming at the production of beauty, the others at the attainment of truth.

Now for every artist who is also a critic or rebel there is a difference of kind between these two sets of conventions. For the purposes of truth the tradition is absolutely indifferent. If, as a matter of fact, the earth goes round the sun, it does so not a whit the less because most ages have believed the opposite. The seeker for truth can, as far as truth is concerned, reject tradition without a qualm. But with art the case is different. Art has to give a message from one man to another. As you can only speak to a man in a language which you both know, so you can only appeal to his artistic side by means of some common tradition. His natural expectation, whether we try to satisfy or to surprise it, to surpass or to disappoint it, is always an essential element in the artistic effect. Consequently the tradition cannot be disregarded.

This distinction is often strongly marked in the practice of different artists. One poet may be both a pioneer of new roads in thought and a breaker of the laws of technique, like Walt Whitman—an enemy of the tradition in both kinds. Another may be slack and anarchical in his technique though quite conventional in his thought. I refrain from suggesting instances. Still more clearly there are poets, such as Shelley or Swinburne, whose works are full of intellectual rebellion while their technique is exquisite and elaborate. The thoughts are bold and strange. The form is the traditional form developed and made more exquisite.

Now Euripides, except for some so-called licences in metre, belongs in my judgment markedly to the last class. In speculation he is a critic and a free lance; in artistic form he is intensely traditional. He seems to have loved the very stiffnesses of the form in which he worked. He developed its inherent powers in ways undreamed of, but he never broke the mould or strayed away into shapelessness or mere realism. His last, and in many respects his greatest, play, the Bacchae, is, as far as our evidence goes, the most formal that he ever wrote.

These, then, are the lights in which we propose to look at Euripides. In attempting to reconstruct his life we must be conscious of two backgrounds against which he will be found standing, according as we regard him as Thinker or as pure Artist. We must first try to understand something of the tradition of thought in which he was reared, that is the general atmosphere of fifth century Athens, and watch how he expressed it and how he reacted against it. Next, we must understand what Greek tragedy was, what rituals and conventions held it firm, and what inner fire kept it living, and so study the method in which Euripides used it for his chosen mode of expression, obeying its laws and at the same time liberating its spirit.

CHAPTER II

THE SOURCES FOR A LIFE OF EURIPIDES: THE MEMORIES REMAINING IN THE FOURTH CENTURY: HIS YOUTH AND ITS SURROUNDINGS: ATHENS AFTER THE PERSIAN WAR: THE GREAT SOPHISTS

It is in one sense impossible to write a life of Euripides, for the simple reason that he lived too long ago. In his time people were only just beginning to write history at all; Herodotus, the "father of history," was his close contemporary. They had begun to record really great events; but it had not occurred to them that the life of any individual was worth all the trouble of tracing out and writing down. Biography of a sort began about two generations afterwards, when the disciples of Aristotle and Epicurus exerted themselves to find out and record the lives of their masters. But biography in our sense—the complete writing of a life year by year with dates and documents—was never practised at all in antiquity. Think of the Gospels, of the Acts, even of Tacitus's Life of Agricola. They are different one from another, but they are all unlike any modern biography in their resolute indifference to anything like completeness. Ancient "Lives" as a rule select a few great deeds, a few great sayings or discourses; they concentrate upon the last years of their subject and often especially upon his death.

The dates at which various eminent men of antiquity died are well known. The man was then famous and his death was a memorable event. But—except in a few aristocratic states, like Cos, which records the actual birthday of the great physician Hippocrates—no baby was eminent and not many young men. Very few dates of birth are known; and in the case of almost all the famous men of antiquity their early histories are forgotten and their early works lost. So it is with Euripides.

History in later antiquity was chiefly a branch of belles lettres and made no great effort after exactness. As a rule it contented itself with the date at which a man "flourished," a very rough conception, conventionally fixed either by the time when he did his most memorable work or the year when he reached the age of forty. The year commonly assigned to Euripides' birth is a good instance of ancient method in these things. The system of chronology was badly confused. In the first place there was no generally accepted era from which to date; and even if there had been, the numerical system, before the invention of Arabic ciphers, was as confused as English spelling is at the present day, and made it hard to do the simplest sums. So the ordinary educational plan was to group events together in some scheme that might not be quite exact but was calculated to have some symbolic interest and to stay in the memory. For instance, the three great tragedians were grouped together round the Battle of Salamis, the great triumph of the Persian Wars in 480 B.C. Aeschylus fought among the heavy-armed infantry, Sophocles danced in a choir of boys to celebrate the victory, and Euripides was born in Salamis on the day of the battle. We do not know the origin of this pleasant fable; but we have another date given in a very ancient chronicle called the Parian Marble, which was found in the island of Paros in the seventeenth century and was composed in the year 264 B.C. It puts the birth of Euripides in 484 B.C., and since we cannot find any reason why this year should be invented, and since the Marble is the oldest witness now extant, we shall probably do well provisionally to accept its statement.

In some of the MSS. which preserve Euripides' plays there are "scholia" or ancient traditional commentaries written round the margin. A few of the oldest notes in them come from Alexandrian scholars who lived in the second century B.C. Others date from Roman times, in the first few centuries of the Christian era; others from the eleventh century and even later. And among them there is a quite ancient document called Life and Race of Euripides.

It is anonymous and shapeless. Sentences may have been added or omitted by the various people who at different times have owned or copied the MSS. But we can see that it is derived from early sources, and notably from a "Life" which was written by one Satyrus, a writer of the Peripatetic or Aristotelian school, towards the end of the third century B.C. Fragments from the same source have been detected in the Latin authors Varro and Gellius; and it has influenced the biographical notice in the ancient Greek lexicon of Suidas (tenth century A.D.). Suidas used also another earlier and better source, the Attic Chronicle of Philochorus.

Philochorus was a careful and systematic annalist of the early third century B.C., who used official documents and verified his statements. His main work was to record all that affected Athens—history, myths, festivals, and customs, but he also wrote various special treatises, one of which was On Euripides. Satyrus wrote a series of Lives of Famous Men, which was very popular, and we are now—since 1911—in a position to judge how undeserved its popularity was. For fragments of his Life of Euripides have been unearthed in Egypt by Drs. Grenfell and Hunt and published in their Oxyrrhyncus Papyri, vol. ix. The life takes the form of a dialogue—apparently a dialogue with a lady. It is a mass of quotations, anecdotes, bits of literary criticism, all run together with an air of culture and pleasantness, a spice of gallantry and a surprising indifference to historical fact. Evidently anecdotes amused Satyrus and facts, as such, did not. He cared about literary style, but he neither cared nor knew about history. The following considerations will make this clear.

Euripides was, more than any other figure in ancient history, a constant butt for the attacks of comedy. And we find, oddly enough, that most of the anecdotes about Euripides in Satyrus are simply the jokes of comedy treated as historical fact. For instance, in Aristophanes' play, The Women at the Thesmophoria, the women, while alone at this private festival, agree to murder Euripides because, by his penetrating study of female character on the stage, he has made life too difficult for them. Euripides, hearing of the plot, persuades his elderly father-in-law to go in disguise to the forbidden celebration and defend him—which he does in a ruinously tactless way. Some scenes of brilliant farce are succeeded by a solemn truce between Euripides and the women of Athens. It shows what our tradition is worth when we find that both the "Life and Race," and Gellius and Satyrus himself, give as sober fact this story which we know—and if we did not know could surely see—to be comic invention. There is another class of fabulous anecdote which plays an even larger part in the Satyrus tradition. In Aristophanes' Frogs (1.1048), in a scene where Euripides is defending his plays against the attacks of Aeschylus, there occurs the chance suggestion that Euripides had learnt from his own experience all the varied villanies of his wicked heroines. The idea took root, and he is represented in the anecdotes as a deceived husband, like his own Theseus or Proetus, and uttering lines suitable to the occasion out of his own tragedies; as having two wives at once, like his own Neoptolemus—one of them named Choirile, or "Piggy," and each of course worse than the other; as torn to pieces by hounds, like his own Actaeon, or by wild women, like his own Pentheus.

Something of this sort is possibly the origin of a famous joke about Euripides' mother, which runs through Aristophanes and is repeated as a fact in all the Lives. We know from Philochorus that it was not true. The joke is to connect her with chervil—a grassy vegetable which grew wild and was only eaten in time of famine—or with wild green-stuff in general, or simply to call her a greengrocer. It was also a joke to say anything about beet-root. (Acharn. 894, Frogs 942), A man begs Euripides to bring

"A new-born chervil from thy mother's breast." (Acharn. 478.)

Or we hear that

"Wild wrongs he works on women,
 Wild as the greens that waved about his cradle." (Thesm. 455.)

When some one is about to quote Euripides his friend cries:

"Don't, don't, for God's sake! Don't be-chervil me!" (Knights 19.)

Now a much-quoted line from Euripides' tragedy Melanippe the Wise runs: "It is not my word but my mother's word"; and we know that Melanippe, and still more her mother, was an authority on potent herbs and simples. Turn his heroine's mother into his own mother and the potent herbs into some absurd vegetable, and the fable is made.

Setting aside this fog of misunderstanding and reckless anecdote, let us try to make out the method on which our best authority, Philochorus, may have put together his account of Euripides. He had almost no written materials; he had no collection of letters and papers such as go to the making of a modern biography. He could, however, consult the public records of tragic performances as collected and edited by Aristotle and his pupils and thus fix the dates of Euripides' plays, especially his first and last performance, his first victory, and the like. He would also find a few public inscriptions in which the poet's name was mentioned, for the archives of that time were mostly engraved on stone and put up in public places. There was also a portrait bust, authentic though slightly idealized, taken in the poet's old age, and showing the worn and beautiful face, the thin hair, and the lips somewhat fallen in. These sources would give him a few skeleton facts; for anything more he would have to depend on the accidental memories that survived. If he wrote about 300-290 B.C. there was no one living who could remember a man who died in 406. But there might be men of seventy whose fathers had spoken to Euripides and whose grandfathers had known him well. Thus he might with luck have struck some vein of intimate and intelligent memory, which would have helped us to understand the great man. But he did not. The memories are all about the poet's old age, and they are all very external. We hear that he wore a long beard and had moles on his face. He lived very much alone, and hated visitors and parties. He had a quantity of books and could not bear women. He lived on the island of Salamis in a cave which had two openings and a beautiful view—a good cave was probably more comfortable than many a Greek house, so this may not have been a great eccentricity—and there you could see him "all day long, thinking to himself and writing, for he simply despised anything that was not great and high." It is like the memories of a child, rather a puzzled child, watching the great man from a distance.

Some few things come out clearly. He lived in his last years with a small knot of intimates. Mnesilochus, his wife's father—or, perhaps, another Mnesilochus of the same family—was a close friend. So was his servant or secretary, Cephisophon. We do not hear of Socrates as an intimate: the two owed a great debt to one another, and we hear that Socrates never went to the theatre except when Euripides had a play performing: to see a Euripides play he would even stir himself so far as to walk all the way to the Piraeus. But it is likely enough that both men were too vivid and original, perhaps too much accustomed to dominate their respective circles, to be quite comfortable in the same room. And we never find Euripides conversing with Socrates in Plato's dialogues.

Some of Euripides' older friends were by this time driven out from Athens. The great "Sophist," Protagoras, had read his famous book, On the Gods, in Euripides' own house. But he was now dead, drowned at sea, and the poet's master, Anaxagoras, had died long before. Some of the younger artists seem to have found a friend in Euripides. There was Timotheus, the young Ionian composer, who—like most musicians of any originality—was supposed to have corrupted the music of the day by his florid style and bold inventions. His first performance in Athens was a mortifying failure, and we are told that the passionate Ionian was on the point of killing himself when the old poet came and encouraged him. He had only to hold fast, and the people who now hissed would turn and applaud.

One fact is especially clear, the restless enmity of the comic writers. Of the eleven comedies of Aristophanes which have come down to us three are largely devoted to Euripides, and not one has managed altogether to avoid touching him. I know of no parallel to it in all the history of literature. Has there ever again been a tragic poet, or any poet, who so centred upon himself year after year till he was nearly eighty the mocking attention of all the popular wits? And how was it that the Athenian public never tired of this incessant poet-baiting, these incessant appeals to literary criticism in the midst of farce? The attacks are sometimes rough and vicious, sometimes acute and searching, often enough they hide a secret admiration. And the chief enemy, Aristophanes, must, to judge from his parodies, have known a large number of Euripides' ninety-two plays by heart, and been at least half fascinated by the object of his satire. However that may be, the hostility of the comic writers had evidently a general hostility behind it. Our tradition states this definitely and the persistency of the attacks proves it. You cannot go on constantly deriding on the stage a person whom your audience does not wish derided. And the unpopularity of Euripides, as we shall see later, is not hard to understand. The Satyrus tradition puts it down to his personal aloofness and austerity. He avoided society, and he "made no effort to please his audience." So that at least he did not soften by personal pleasantness the opposition they felt to his whole view of life. It was not only that he was utterly alienated from the War Party and the mob leaders: here he only agreed with Aristophanes. It was that he had pierced through to a deeper stratum of thought, in which most of the pursuits and ideals of the men about him stood condemned. Socrates reached the same plane, and they killed Socrates.

It is somewhat harder to understand the universal assumption of our authorities that Euripides was a notorious castigator of the female sex and that the women of Athens naturally hated him. To us he seems an aggressive champion of women; more aggressive, and certainly far more appreciative, than Plato. Songs and speeches from the Medea are recited to-day at suffragist meetings. His tragic heroines are famous and are almost always treated with greater interest and insight than his heroes. Yet not only the ancients, but all critics up to the last generation or so, have described him as a woman-hater. What does it mean? Is Aristophanes ironical, and are the scholiasts and grammarians merely stupid? Or is there some explanation for this extraordinary judgment?

I think the explanation is that the present age is the first, or almost the first, that has learned to treat its heroines in fiction as real human beings, with what are called "mixed characters." As lately as the time of Sir Walter Scott, perhaps as lately as Dickens, common convention demanded that a heroine, if sympathetic, should be so free from faults as to be almost without character. Ibsen's heroines, who were real human beings studied with sympathy but with profound sincerity, seemed to their generation shocking and even horrible. All through the ages the ideal of womanhood in conventional fiction has mostly been of the type praised by one great Athenian thinker: "the greatest glory for a woman is to be as little mentioned as possible among men." If that ideal was really predominant among the women of Athens, it is no wonder that they felt outraged by Euripides. They had not reached, and most of their husbands had not reached, the point of being interested in good study of character, much less the point of demanding a freer and more strenuous life. To the average stupid Athenian it was probably rather wicked for a woman to have any character, wicked for her to wish to take part in public life, wicked for her to acquire learning, or to doubt any part of the conventional religion, just as it was wicked for her to deceive her husband. Such women should not be spoken about; above all they should not be treated with understanding and sympathy. The understanding made it all infinitely worse. To people of this type the women of Euripides must have been simply shocking and the poet himself a cruel enemy of the sex. One only wonders that they could stand Sophocles' heroines, such as Antigone and Jocasta. To cleverer men, like Aristophanes, the case would, no doubt, seem rather more complicated. But Aristophanes, amid the many flashes of sympathy he shows for "advanced" women, was not the man to go against his solid conservative audience or to forgo such rich material for jokes.

In any case this is the kind of picture we have of Euripides in his last years; a figure solitary, austere, with a few close intimates, wrapped up in living for what he would call "the service of the Muses," in music, poetry and speculation; capable still of thrilling his audiences with an intensity of tragic emotion such as no other poet had ever reached; but bowed with age, somewhat friendless, and like other solitaries a little strange in his habits; uncomprehendingly admired and hated, and moving always through a mist of half-envious, half-derisive laughter. Calvus et calvinista—one is reminded, amid many differences, of the quaint words in which William the Silent describes his own passage from youth to age, till the brilliant Catholic prince, leader of courts and tourneys, sate at last in his lonely council chamber "bald and a Calvinist." Let us try to trace the path of life which led him to this end.

He was the son of Mnesarchus or Mnesarchides—such names often have alternative forms—who is said to have been a merchant. His mother, Cleito, the supposed greengrocer, was, according to Philochorus, "of very high birth." He was born at Phlya, a village in the centre of Attica. The neighbourhood is celebrated still for its pleasant trees and streams in the midst of a sunburnt land. In Euripides' time it was more famous for its temples. It was the seat of Demeter Anesidora (Earth, Upsender of Gifts), of Dionysus of the Blossom, and the Dread Virgins, old-world and mysterious names, not like the prevailing gods of the Homeric mythology. Most famous of all, it possessed the mystery temple of Erôs, or Love. Owing to the researches of recent years, these mysteries can now be in their general nature understood. They are survivals of an old tribal society, in which all the boys as they reached maturity were made to pass through certain ordeals and initiations. They were connected both with vegetation and with re-birth after death, because they dated from a remote age in which the fruitfulness of the tribal fields was not differentiated from the fruitfulness of the flocks and the human families, and the new members born into the community were normally supposed to be the old ancestors returning to their homes. By Euripides' day such beliefs had faded into mystical doctrines, to be handled with speechless reverence, not to be questioned or understood, but they had their influence upon his mind. There were other temples too, belonging to the more aristocratic gods of heroic mythology, as embodied in Homer. Euripides was in his youth cup-bearer to a certain guild of Dancers—dancing in ancient times had always religious associations about it—who were chosen from the "first families in Athens" and danced round the altar of the Delian Apollo. He was also Fire-bearer to the Apollo of Cape Zôstêr; that is, it was his office to carry a torch in the procession which on a certain night of each year met the Delian Apollo at Cape Zôstêr, and escorted him on his mystic path from Delos to Athens.

When the child was four years old he had to be hurried away from his home and then from his country. The Persians were coming. The awful words lost none of their terror from the fact that in Greek the word "Persai," Persians, meant "to destroy." So later it added something to the dread inspired by Rome that her name, "Roma," meant "strength." The family must have crossed the narrow seas to Salamis or further, and seen the smoke of the Persian conflagrations rising daily from new towns and villages of Attica and at last from the Acropolis, or Citadel, itself. Then came the enormous desperate sea-battle; the incredible victory; the sight of the broken oriental fleet beating sullenly away for Asia and safety, and the solemn exclamation of the Athenian general, Themistocles, "It is not we who have done this!" The next year the Athenians could return to Attica and begin to build up their ruined farms. Then came the final defeat of the Persian land army at Plataea, and the whole atmosphere lifted. Athens felt that she had acted like a hero and was reaping a hero's reward. She had borne the full brunt of the war; she had voluntarily put herself under the orders of Sparta rather than risk a split in the Greek forces; and now she had come out as the undisputed mistress of the sea, the obvious champion round whom the eastern Greeks must rally. Sparta, not interested in matters outside her own borders, and not capable of any constructive policy, dropped sulkily out, and left her to carry on the offensive war for the liberation of the Greeks in Asia. The current of things was with her.

But this great result was not merely the triumph of a particular city; it was the triumph of an ideal and a way of life. Freedom had defeated despotism, democracy had defeated kings, hardy poverty had defeated all the gold of the East. The men who fought of their free will for home and country had proved more lasting fighters than the conscripts who were kept in the lines by fear of tortures and beheadings and impalements. Above all "virtue," as the Greeks called it, or "virtue" and "wisdom" together, had shown their power. The words raise a smile in us; indeed, our words do not properly correspond with the Greek, because we can not get our ideas simple enough. "Virtue" is what makes a man, or anything else, good; it is the quality of a good soldier, a good general, a good citizen, a good bootmaker, a good horse or almost a good sword. And "wisdom" is that by which a man knows how to do things—to use a spear, or a tool, to think and speak and write, to do figures and history and geometry, to advise and convince his fellow-citizens. All these great forces moved, or so it seemed at the time, in the same direction; and probably it was hardly felt as a dangerous difference when many people preferred to say that it was "piety" that had won in the war against "impiety," and that the Persians had been destroyed because, being monotheists, they had denied the Gods. No doubt "piety," properly understood, was a kind of "wisdom." Let us take a few passages from the old Ionian historian, Herodotus, to illustrate what the feeling for Athens was in Euripides' youth.

Athens represented Hellenism. (Hdt. I. 60.) "The Greek race was distinguished of old from the barbarian as more intelligent and more emancipated from silly nonsense (or 'savagery') . . . And of all the Greeks the Athenians were counted first in Wisdom." Athens, as the old epigram put it, was "The Hellas of Hellas."

And this superior wisdom went with freedom and democracy. "So Athens grew. It is clear wherever you test it, what a good thing is equality among men. Athens under the tyrants was no better than her neighbours, even in war; when freed from the tyrants she was far the first of all." (V. 78.)

And what did this freedom and democracy mean? A speaker in Herodotus tells us (III. 80): "A tyrant disturbs ancient laws, violates women, kills men without trial. But a people ruling—first the very name of it is beautiful, and secondly a people does none of these things."

And the freedom is not mere licence. When Xerxes heard the small numbers of the Greeks who were opposed to him he asked why they did not all run away, "especially as you say they are free and there is no one to stop them?" And the Spartan answered: "They are free, O King, but not free to do everything. For there is a master over them named Law, whom they fear more than thy servants fear thee." (VII. 104. This refers specially to the Spartans, but the same tale is told by Aeschylus of the Athenians. It applies to any free Greeks as against the enslaved barbarian.)

The free Athenian must also have aretê, "virtue." He must be a better man in all senses than the common herd. As Themistocles put it; at every turn of life there is a choice between a higher and a lower, and they must choose the higher always. Especially there is one sense in which Athens must profess aretê; the sense of generosity or chivalry. When the various Greek states were contending for the leadership before the battle of Artemisium, the Athenians, though contributing much the largest fleet, "thought that the great thing was that Greece should be saved, and gave up their claims." (Hdt. VIII. 3.) In the similar dispute for the post of honour and danger, before the battle of Plataea, the Athenians did plead their cause and won it. But they pleaded promising to abide loyally by Sparta's decision if their claims were rejected, and their arguments show what ideal they had formed of themselves. They claim that in recent years they alone have met the Persians single-handed on behalf of all Greece; that in old times it was they who gave refuge to the children of Heracles when hunted through Greece by the tyrant Eurystheus; it was they who, at the cost of war, prevented the conquering Thebans from leaving their dead enemies to rot unburied and thus offending against the laws of Greece and humanity.

This is the light in which Athens conceived herself; the ideal up to which, amid much confused, hot-headed and self-deceiving patriotism, she strove to live. She was to be the Saviour of Hellas.

Euripides was about eight when the ruined walls of Athens were rebuilt and the city, no longer defenceless against her neighbours, could begin to rebuild the "House of Athena" on the Acropolis and restore the Temples and the Festivals throughout Attica. He can hardly have been present when the general Themistocles, then at the height of his fame, provided the Chorus for the earliest of the great tragedians, Phrynichus, in 476 B.C. But he must have watched the new paintings being put up by the same Themistocles in the temples at Phlya, with scenes from the Persian War. And through his early teens he must have watched the far more famous series of pictures with which Polygnôtus, the first of the great Greek painters, was adorning the Acropolis; pictures that canonized scenes from the Siege of Troy and other legendary history. When he was ten he may probably have seen a curious procession which brought back from the island of Skyros the bones of Theseus, the mythical king of Athens and the accepted symbol, king though he was, of Athenian enlightenment and democracy. Athens was now too great and too self-conscious to allow Theseus to lie on foreign soil. When he was twelve he may have seen Aeschylus' Persae, "the one great play dealing with an historical event that exists in literature." When he was seventeen he pretty certainly saw the Seven against Thebes and was much influenced by it; but the Choregus this time was a new statesman, Pericles. Themistocles was in banishment; and the other great heroes of the Persian time, Aristides and Miltiades, dead.

Next year, 466 B.C. Euripides became officially an "Ephêbus," or "Youth." He was provided with a shield and spear, and set to garrison and police duty in the frontier forts of Attica. Full military service was to follow in two years. Meantime the current of his thoughts must have received a shock. For, while his shield and spear were still fresh, news came of one of the most stunning military disasters in Athenian history. A large colony which had been established on the river Strymon in Thrace had been lured into dangerous country by the Thracian tribes, then set upon by overwhelming numbers and massacred to the number of ten thousand. No wonder that one of Euripides' earliest plays, when he took to writing, was the story of Rhesus, the Thracian, and his rushing hordes of wild tribesmen.

But meantime Euripides had not found his work in life. We hear that he was a good athlete; there were records of his prize-winning in Athens and in Eleusis. Probably every ambitious boy in Greece did a good deal of running and boxing. More serious was his attempt at painting. Polygnôtus was at work in Athens, and the whole art advancing by leaps and bounds. He tried to find his true work there, and paintings by his hand were discovered by antiquarians of later times—or so they believed—in the town of Megara. His writings show a certain interest in painting here and there, and it is perhaps the painter in him that worked out in the construction of his dramas such fine and varied effects of grouping.

But there was more in the air than painting and sculpture. The youth of Euripides fell in an age which saw perhaps the most extraordinary intellectual awakening known to human history. It had been preparing for about a century in certain cities of Ionian Greece, on the coast of Asia Minor, rich and cultivated states, subject for the most part to Lydian or Persian governors. The revolt of these cities and its suppression by Persia had sent numbers of Ionian "wise men," philosophers, poets, artists, historians, men of science, to seek for refuge in Greece, and especially in Athens. Athens was held to be the mother-city of all the Ionian colonies, and had been their only champion in the revolt. She became now, as one of these Ionian exiles put it, "the hearth on which the fire of Hellas burned." It is difficult to describe this great movement in a few pages, but one can, perhaps, get some idea of it by an imaginary comparison. Imagine first the sort of life that was led in remote parts of Yorkshire or Somerset towards the end of the eighteenth century, a stagnant rustic life with no moving ideas, and unquestioning in its obedience to authority, in which hardly any one could read except the parson, and the parson's reading was not of a kind to stir a man's pulse. And next imagine the intellectual ferment which was then in progress in London or Paris; the philosophers, painters, historians and men of science, the voices proclaiming that all men were equal, that the laws of England were unjust to the poor, that slavery was a crime, and that monarchy was a false form of government, or that no action was morally wrong except what tended to produce human misery. Imagine then what would occur in the mind of a clever and high-thinking boy who was brought suddenly from the one society into the heart of the second, and made to realise that the battles and duties and prizes of life were tenfold more thrilling and important than he had ever dreamed. That is the kind of awakening that must have occurred in the minds of a large part of the Greek people in the early fifth century.

A thoroughly backward peasant in a Greek village—even an Attic village like Phlya—had probably as few ideas as other uneducated peasants. In Athens some fifty years later we hear that it was impossible, with the best will in the world, to find any one who could not read or write. (Ar. Knights 188 ff.) But the difference in time and place is cardinal. The countryman who voted for the banishment of Aristides the Just had to ask some one else to write the name for him. Such a man did not read nor yet think. He more or less hated the next village and regarded its misfortunes as his own advantage. He was sunk in superstition. His customs were rigid and not understood. He might worship a goddess with a horse's head or a hero with a snake's tail. He would perform for the welfare of his fields traditional sacrifices that were often filthy and sometimes cruel. On certain holy days he would tear small beasts to pieces or drive them into a fire; in very great extremities he would probably think no medicine so good as human blood. His rules of agriculture would be a mixture of rough common sense and stupid taboos: he would not reap till the Pleiades were rising, and he would carefully avoid sitting on a fixed stone. When he sought for learning, he would get it in old traditional books like Hesiod, which taught him how Ouranos had been mutilated by his son Cronos, and Cronos bound with chains by his son Zeus; how Zeus was king of gods and men, but had been cheated by Prometheus into accepting bones instead of meat in a sacrifice. He would believe that Tantalus had given the gods his son Pelops to eat, to see if they would know the difference, and some of them had eaten bits of him. He would perhaps be ready, with great hesitation, to tolerate certain timid attempts to expurgate the story, like Pindar's, for instance, which results, according to our judgment, in making it rather worse. And this man, rooted in his customs, his superstitions, his narrow-minded cruelties, will of course regard every departure from his own way of life as so much pure wickedness. In every contest that goes on between Intelligence and Stupidity, between Enlightenment and Obscurantism, the powers of the dark have this immense advantage: they never understand their opponents, and consequently represent them as always wrong, always wicked, whereas the intelligent party generally makes an effort to understand the stupid and to sympathize with anything that is good or fine in their attitude. Many of our Greek Histories still speak as if the great spiritual effort which created fifth century Hellenism was a mass of foolish chatter and intellectual trickery and personal self-indulgence.

It was not that, nor anything like that. Across the mind of our stupid peasant the great national struggle against Persia brought first the idea that perhaps really it was better to die than to be a slave; that it was well to face death not merely for his own home but actually—incredible as it seemed—for other people's homes, for the homes of those wretched people in the next village. Our own special customs and taboos, he would reflect with a shiver, do not really matter when they are brought into conflict with a common Hellenism or a common humanity. There are greater things about us than we knew. There are also greater men. These men who are in everybody's mouth: Themistocles above all, who has defeated the Persian and saved Greece: but crowds of others besides, Aristides the Just and Miltiades, the hero of Marathon; Demokêdes, the learned physician, who was sought out by people in need of help from Italy to Susa; Hecataeus, who had made a picture of the whole earth, showing all the countries and cities and rivers and how far each is from the next, and who could have saved the Ionians if they had only listened to him; Pythagoras, who had discovered all about numbers and knew the wickedness of the world and had founded a society, bound by strict rules, to combat it. What is it about these men that has made them so different from you and me and the other farmers who meet in the agora on market-day? It is sophia, wisdom; it is aretê, virtue. They are not a bit stronger in the arm, not bigger, not richer, or more high-born: they are just wiser, and thus better men. Cannot we be made wise? We know we are stupid, we are very ignorant, but we can learn.

The word Sophistes means either "one who makes wise," or, possibly, as some scholars think, "one who deals in wisdom." The difference is slight. In any case it was in answer to this call for sophia that the Sophists arose. Doubtless they were of all kinds; great men and small, honest and dishonest; teachers of real wisdom and of pretence. Our tradition is rather bitter against them, because it dates from the bitter time of reaction and disappointment, when the hopes of the fifth century and the men who guided it seemed to have led Athens only to her fall. Plato in particular is against them as he is against Athens herself. In the main the judgment of the afterworld upon them will depend on the side we take in a never-ending battle: they fought for light and knowledge and freedom and the development of all man's powers. If we prefer blinkers and custom, subordination and the rod, we shall think them dangerous and shallow creatures. But, to see what the sophists were like, let us consider two of them who are recorded as having specially been the teachers of Euripides.

Anaxagoras of Clazomenae, in Ionia, was about fifteen years older than Euripides, and spent some thirty years of his life in Athens. He discovered for the first time that the moon shines by the reflection of the sun's light; and he explained, in the main correctly, the cause of eclipses. The sun was not a god: it was a white-hot mass of stone or earth, in size perfectly enormous. In describing its probable size, language failed him; he only got as far as saying—what must have seemed almost a mad exaggeration—that it was many times larger than the Peloponnese. He held, if he did not invent, a particular form of the atomic theory which has played such a great rôle in the history of modern science. He was emphatic on the indestructibility of matter. Things could be broken up into their elements and could grow together again, but nothing could be created or destroyed. There was order in the world and purpose, and this was the work of a conscious power which he called "Nous," or Mind. "All things were together in a mass, till Mind came and put order into them." Mind is outside things, not mixed with them, and some authorities say that Anaxagoras called it "God." Meantime, he showed by experiment the reality and substance of air, and disproved the common notion of "empty space." It will be seen that these ideas, if often crudely expressed, are essentially the same ideas which gave new life to modern science after the sleep of the Middle Ages. Almost every one of them is the subject of active dispute at the present day.

Apart from physical science, we learn that Anaxagoras was a close friend and adviser of the great Athenian statesman, Pericles; and we have by chance an account of a long discussion between the two men about the theory of punishment—whether the object of it is to do "justice" upon a wrong-doer apart from any result that may accrue, or simply to deter others from doing the same and thus make society better. The question is the subject of a vigorous correspondence in the Times while these words are writing. We can understand what an effect such a teacher as this would have on the eager young man from Phlya. One great word of liberation was already in the air and belongs to no one sophist or philosopher. This was the distinction between Nature on the one hand and Custom or Convention on the other. The historian Herodotus, who was no sophist but loved a good story, tells how the Persian king, Darius, called some Greeks and some Indian tribesmen together into his presence. He then asked the Greeks what payment would induce them to eat the dead bodies of their fathers. "Nothing in the world," they cried in indignation. "They would reverently burn them." He proceeded to ask the Indians what they would take to burn their fathers' bodies, and they repelled the bare thought with horror; they would do nothing but eat them with every mark of love and respect. "Fire burns in the same way both here and in Persia," the saying was, "but men's notions of right and wrong are not at all the same." The one is Nature; the other is man's Custom or Convention. This antithesis between "Phusis" and "Nomos" ran vividly through the whole of Greek philosophy, and awoke with renewed vigour in Rousseau and the radical writers of the eighteenth century. It is an antithesis against which conformist dialecticians have always turned their sharpest weapons. It has again and again been dissected and refuted and shown to be philosophically untenable: but it still lives and has still something of the old power to shatter and to set free. All the thinkers of Greece at the time we are treating were testing the laws and maxims of their day, and trying to find out what really rested on Nature and what was the mere embroidery of man. It is always a dangerous and exciting inquiry; especially because the most irrational conventions are apt also to be the most sacrosanct.

This whole spirit was specially incarnate in another of Euripides' teachers. We hear of Protagoras in his old age from that enemy of the sophists, Plato. But for this sophist even Plato's satire is kindly and almost reverent. Protagoras worked not at physical science, but at language and philosophy. He taught men to think and speak; he began the study of grammar by dividing sentences into four kinds, Optative, Interrogative, Indicative, Imperative. He taught rhetoric; he formulated the first theory of democracy. But it was as a sceptic that he struck men's imaginations most. "About the Gods, I have no means of knowing either that they are or are not. For the hindrances to knowledge are many, the darkness of the subject and the shortness of man's life." Numbers of people, no doubt, went as far as this, and without suffering for it as Protagoras did; but his scepticism cut deeper and raised questions still debated in modern thought. "Man is the measure of things"; there is no truth to be had beyond the impression made on a man's mind. When this given object seems one thing to A and another thing to B, it is to each one exactly what it seems; just as honey not only seems sweet but is sweet to a healthy man, and not only seems bitter but is bitter to a man with jaundice. Then you can not say, we may ask, that one or other impression is false, and will prove false on further inquiry? No: he answers; each impression is equally true. The only difference is that each state of mind is not equally good. You cannot prove to the jaundiced man that his honey is sweet, for it is not: or to the drunkard that he does not desire his drink, for he does: what you can do is to alter the men's state of mind, to cure the jaundice or the drunkenness. Our cognition flows and changes. It is the result of an active impact upon a passive percipient. And, resulting from this change, there are in practice always two things to be said, a pro and a con. about every possible proposition. There is no general statement that cannot be contradicted.

Other teachers also are represented as having influenced Euripides; Archelaus, who tried to conceive Anaxagoras's "Mind" in some material form, as air or spirit—for spiritus, of course, means "breath"; Prodicus, who, besides his discoveries in grammar, is the author of a popular and edifying fable which has served in many schoolrooms for many centuries. It tells how Heracles once came to some cross roads, one road open, broad, and smooth and leading a little downhill, the other narrow and uphill and rough: and on the first you gradually became a worse and worse man, on the second a better one. There was Diogenes of Apollonia, whose theories about air seem to have had some effect on Euripides' writings; and of course there was, among the younger men, Socrates. Socrates is too great and too enigmatic a teacher to be summed up in a few sentences, and though a verse of ancient comedy has come down to us, saying, "Socrates piles the faggots for Euripides' fire," his influence on his older friend is not very conspicuous. Euripides must have caught something from his scepticism, his indifference to worldly standards, his strong purpose, and something also from his resolute rejection of all philosophy except that which was concerned with the doings and feelings of men. "The fields and trees will not talk to me; it is only the human beings in the city that will." That saying of Socrates might be the motto of many a dramatist.

The greatness of these philosophers or sophists of the fifth century does not, of course, lie in the correctness of their scientific results. The dullest and most unilluminated text-book produced at the present day is far more correct than Anaxagoras. Their greatness lies partly in the pioneer quality of their work. They first struck out the roads by which later workers could advance further. Partly in the daring and felicity with which they hit upon great and fruitful ideas, ideas which have brought light and freedom with them whenever they have recurred to men's minds, and which, as we have seen, are to a great extent still, after more than two thousand years, living issues in philosophic thought. Partly it lies in the mere freedom of spirit with which they set to work, unhampered by fears and taboos, to seek the truth, to create beauty, and to improve human life. The difference of atmosphere between the sophists of the Periclean circle and the ordinary backward Attic farmer must have been visible to every observer. If more evidence of the great gulf was needed, it was supplied emphatically enough in the experience of Euripides. He was himself prosecuted by Cleon, the demagogue, for "impiety." The same charge had been levelled even against his far less destructive predecessor, Aeschylus. Of these three special friends whom we have mentioned, Euripides did not live to see Socrates condemned to death and executed. But he saw Anaxagoras, in spite of the protection of Pericles, accused of "impiety" and compelled to fly for his life. He saw Protagoras, for the book which he had read aloud in Euripides' own house, prosecuted and condemned. The book was publicly burned; the author escaped, it is said, only to be drowned at sea, a signal mark in the eyes of the orthodox of how the gods regarded such philosophy.

Thought was no doubt freer in ancient Athens than in any other city within two thousand years of it. Those who suffered for religious advance are exceedingly few. But it was not in human nature, especially in such early times, for individuals to do such great service to their fellow men and not occasionally be punished for it. They induced men for a time to set reason and high ideals above the instincts of the herd: and sooner or later the herd must turn and trample them.

One of the ancient lives says that it was this sense of the antagonism between Anaxagoras and the conservative masses that turned Euripides away from philosophy. One need scarcely believe that. The way he took was not the way to escape from danger or unpopularity. And when a man shows extraordinary genius for poetry one need not search for the reasons which induced him not to write prose. He followed in the wake not of Anaxagoras but of Aeschylus.

CHAPTER III

LIFE CONTINUED: WHAT IS A GREEK TRAGEDY? EURIPIDES' EARLY PLAYS: "ALCESTIS" AND "TELEPHUS"

To the public of the present day a play is merely an entertainment, and it was the same to the Elizabethans. Shakespeare can say to his audience "Our true intent is all for your delight," and we feel no particular shock in reading the words. The companies were just noblemen's servants; and it was natural enough that if Lord Leicester's players did not amuse Lord Leicester's guests, they should be sent away and others hired. If they too proved dull, the patron could drop the play altogether and call for tumblers and dancing dogs.

To a playwright of the twelfth century, who worked out in the church or in front of it his presentation of the great drama of the Gospel, such an attitude would have seemed debased and cynical. However poor the monkish players or playwright might be, surely that which they were presenting was in itself enough to fill the mind of a spectator. To them, as the great mediævalist, Gaston Paris, puts it, "the universe was a vast stage, on which was played an eternal drama, full of tears and joy, its actors divided between heaven, earth and hell; a drama whose end is foreseen, whose changes of fortune are directed by the hand of God, yet whose every scene is rich and thrilling." The spectator was admitted to the councils of the Trinity; he saw the legions of darkness mingling themselves with the lives of humanity, tempting and troubling, and the saints and angels at their work of protection or intercession; he saw with his own eyes the kiss of Judas, the scourging and crucifixion, the descent into Hell, the resurrection and ascension; and, lastly, the dragging down to red and bloody torment of the infinite multitudes of the unorthodox or the wicked. Imagine what passed in the minds of those who witnessed in full faith such a spectacle! [*Poésie du Moyen Age I, Essay I.*]

Now, in spite of a thousand differences of social organization and religious dogma, the atmosphere of primitive Greek tragedy must have been most strangely similar to this. It is not only that, like the mediæval plays, Greek tragedy was religious; that it was developed out of a definite ritual; not even that the most marked links of historical continuity can be traced between the death-and-resurrection ritual of certain Pagan "saviours" and those of the mediæval drama. It is that the ritual on which tragedy was based embodied the most fundamental Greek conceptions of life and fate, of law and sin and punishment.

When we say that tragedy originated in a dance, ritual or magical, intended to represent the death of the vegetation this year and its coming return in triumph next year, the above remarks may seem hard to justify. But we must remember several things. First, a dance was in ancient times essentially religious, not a mere capering with the feet but an attempt to express with every limb and sinew of the body those emotions for which words, especially the words of simple and unlettered men, are inadequate (see p. 229). Again, vegetation is to us an abstract common noun; to the ancient it was a personal being, not "it" but "He." His death was as our own deaths, and his re-birth a thing to be anxiously sought with prayers and dances. For if He were not re-born, what would happen? Famine, and wholesale death by famine, was a familiar thought, a regularly returning terror, in these primitive agricultural villages. Nay, more, why must the cycle of summer and winter roll as it does? Why must "He" die and men die? Some of the oldest Greek philosophers have no doubt about the answer: there has been "Hubris" or "Adikia," Pride or Injustice, and the result thereof must needs be death. Every year He waxes too strong and commits "Hubris," and such sin has its proper punishment. "The sun shall not transgress his measures," says Heraclitus; "if he does he shall be pursued by Erinyes, till justice be re-fulfilled." It is the law of all existing things. "They all pay retribution for injustice, one to another, according to the Ordinance of Time" (Heraclitus, fr. 94, Anaximander, fr. 9). And the history of each year's bloom was an example of this refluent balance. The Year Daemon—Vegetation Spirit or Corn God or whatever we call him—waxes proud and is slain by his enemy, who becomes thereby a murderer and must in turn perish at the hands of the expected avenger, who is at the same time the Wronged One re-risen. The ritual of this Vegetation Spirit is extraordinarily wide-spread in all quarters of the globe, and may best be studied in Dr. Frazer's Golden Bough, especially in the part entitled, "The Dying God." Dionysus, the daemon of tragedy, is one of these Dying Gods, like Attis, Adonis, Osiris.

The Dionysiac ritual which lay at the back of tragedy, may be conjectured in its full form to have had six regular stages: an Agôn or Contest, in which the Dæmon fights against his enemy, who—since it is really this year fighting last year—is apt to be almost identical with himself; a Pathos, or disaster, which very commonly takes the shape of a "Sparagmos," or Tearing in pieces; the body of the Corn God being scattered in innumerable seeds over the earth; sometimes of some other sacrificial death; (3) a Messenger, who brings the news; a Lamentation, very often mixed with a Song of Rejoicing, since the death of the Old King is also the accession of the new; the Discovery or Recognition of the hidden or dismembered god; and his Epiphany or Resurrection in glory.

[Footnote 1: The above is the present writer's re-statement, published in Miss Harrison's Themis, pp. 341 ff., of the orthodox view of the origin of tragedy. See also Cornford From Religion to Philosophy, first few chapters. The chief non-Dionysiac theory is Professor Ridgeway's, who derives tragedy directly from the funeral cult of individual heroes: Origin of Tragedy, Cambridge, 1910.]

This ritual of Dionysus, being made into a drama and falling into the hands of a remarkable set of creative artists, developed into what we know as Greek tragedy. The creative passion of the artist gradually conquered the emotion of the mere worshipper.

Exactly the same development took place in mediæval drama, or rather it was taking place when new secular influences broke in and destroyed it. The liturgical plays first enacted the main story of the New Testament; then they emphasized particular parts—there is a beautiful play, for instance, on the Massacre of the Innocents; then they developed imaginatively scenes that are implied but not mentioned in the Gospel, such as the experiences of the Magdalen when she lived "in joy," her dealings with cosmetic-sellers and the like; then, ranging right outside the Gospel histories, they dealt with the lives of St. Nicholas, St. Antony or any person who provided a good legend and had some claim to an atmosphere of sanctity.

In the same way Greek tragedy extended its range first to embrace the histories of other Heroes or Daemons—the difference is slight—who were essentially like Dionysus: Pentheus, Lycurgus, Hippolytus, Actaeon and especially, I should be inclined to add, Orestes. Then it took in any heroes to whose memory some ritual was attached. For the play is, with the rarest and most doubtful exceptions, essentially the enactment of a ritual, or rather of what the Greeks called an "aition"—that is, a supposed historical event which is the origin or "cause" of the ritual. Thus the death of Hippolytus is the "aition" of the lamentation-rite performed at the grave of Hippolytus; the death of Aias is the "aition" of the festival called Aianteia; the death of Medea's children, the "aition" of a certain ritual at Corinth; the story of Prometheus the "aition" of a certain Fire-festival in Athens. The tragedy, as ritual, enacts its own legendary origin.

There is then a further extension of the theme, to include a very few events in recent history. But we must observe that only those events were chosen which were felt to have about them some heroic grandeur or mystery; I think we may even say, only those events which, like the Battle of Salamis or the Fall of Miletus, had been made the subject of some religious celebration.

However that may be, the general temper of tragedy moved strongly away from the monotony of fixed ritual. The subjects thus grew richer and more varied; the mode of representation loftier and more artistic. What had begun as almost pure ritual ended by being almost pure drama. By the time Euripides began to write the master-tragedian Aeschylus had already lifted Greek drama to its highest level: whole generations have read his plays without even suspecting the ritual form that lies behind them. Aeschylus had also made the whole performance much longer and more impressive: he composed three continuous tragedies forming a single whole and followed by the strange performance called a Satyr-play. The wild element of revelry which was proper to Dionysus worship, with its bearded dancing half-animal satyrs, had been kept severely away from the stage during the three tragedies and must burst in to have its fling when they were finished. The other tragedians do not seem to have written in trilogies, and Euripides at any rate moved gradually away from satyr-plays. In their stead he put a curious sort of pro-satyric tragedy, a play in the tragic convention and free from the satyric coarseness, but containing at least one half-comic figure and preserving some fantastic quality of atmosphere.

On the Great Festival of Dionysus each year—and sometimes on other festivals—this ritual of tragedy was solemnly performed in the theatre of the god. Like most Greek festivals the performance took the form of a competition. The ground of this custom was, I suspect, religious. It was desired to get a spirit of "Nikê," or victory, into the celebration, and you could only get this by means of a contest. The Archon, or magistrate, in charge of the festival selected three poets to compete, and three rich men to be their "Chorêgoi," that is, to provide all the expenses of the performance. The poet was then said to have "obtained a chorus," and his work now was to "teach the chorus." At the end of the festival a body of five judges, somewhat elaborately and curiously chosen, awarded a first, second and third prize. Even the last competitor must have a kind of "victory"; any mention of "failure" at such a time would be ill-omened.

This, in rough outline, was the official mould in which our poet's creative activity had to run. The record of his early work is, as we had reason to expect, terribly defective. But we do happen to know the name and subject of the first play for which he "was granted a chorus." It was called the Daughters of Pelias. Its story was based on the old ritual of the Year-god, who is cut to pieces or scattered like the seed, and then restored to life and youth. Medea, the enchantress maiden from the further shores of the Friendless Sea, had fled from her home with the Greek adventurer Jason, the winner of the Golden Fleece. She came with him to Thessaly, where his uncle Pelias was king. Pelias had usurped Jason's ancestral crown and therefore hated him. The daughters of Pelias doubtless sneered at Medea and encouraged Jason's growing distaste for his barbarian prize. The savage woman determined at one blow to be rid of Pelias, to punish his daughters, and reconquer Jason's love. She had the power of renovating the life of the old. She persuaded the daughters of Pelias to try her method on their father, with the result that he died in agony, and they stood guilty of a hideous murder. Medea, we may conjecture, was triumphant, till she found she had made Jason a ruined man and taught him really to hate her. The play is characteristic in two ways. It was clearly based on the old ritual, and it treated one of Euripides' great subjects, the passions of a suffering and savage woman.

The Daughters of Pelias was produced in 455, when the poet was twenty-nine, just a year after the death of Aeschylus and thirteen years after the first victory of Sophocles. Euripides' own first victory—we do not know the name of the successful play—did not come till 442, a year before Sophocles' masterpiece, the Antigone.

We have only two examples, and those not certain, of Euripides' work before that time. The Cyclops is a satyr-play pure and simple, and the only complete specimen of its class. It is probably earlier than the Alcestis, and is interesting because it shows Euripides writing for once without any arrière pensée, or secondary intention. It is a gay and grotesque piece, based on Homer's story of Odysseus in the Cyclops' cave. The farcical and fantastic note is firmly held, so that the climax of the story, in which the monster's eye is burnt out with a log of burning wood, is kept unreal and not disgusting. The later Euripides would probably have made it horrible and swung our sympathies violently round to the side of the victim.

The Rhesus has come down to us in a very peculiar condition and is often considered spurious. We know, however, that Euripides wrote a Rhesus, and tradition says that he was "very young" when he wrote it. My own view—explained in the preface to my translation—would make it probably a very early pro-satyric play which was produced after the poet's death and considerably rewritten. It is a young man's play, full of war and adventure, of spies in wolf-skins and white chargers and gallant chivalry. That is not much like the Euripides whom we know elsewhere; but his mark is upon the last scene, in which the soldiers stand embarrassed and silent while a solitary mother weeps over her dead son. The poetry of the scene is exquisite; but what is most characteristic is the sudden flavour of bitterness, the cold wind that so suddenly takes the heart out of joyous war. Some touch of that bitter flavour will be found hereafter in every play, however beautiful or romantic, that comes from the pen of Euripides.

Up to the year 438, when the poet was forty-six, the records, as we have said, almost fail us. But in that year he produced a set of four plays, The Cretan Women, Alcmaeon in Psôphis, Telephus, and, in place of a satyr-play, the Alcestis. The last is still extant and is very characteristic of the master's mind. The saga told how Admetus, a king in Thessaly, was fated to die on a certain day, but, in return for his piety of old, was allowed to find a substitute to die for him. His old father and mother refused; his young wife, Alcestis, gladly consented to die. Amid exquisite songs of mourning she is carried to her grave, when the wild hero, Heracles, comes to the house seeking hospitality. Admetus, with primitive courtesy, conceals what has happened and orders him to be given entertainment. The burial is finished when Heracles, already revelling and drunken and crowned with flowers, learns the truth. Sobered at the touch he goes out into the night to wrestle with Death amid the tombs and crush his ribs for him till he yields up his prey. One sees the fantastic satyr note. The play is not truly tragic; it touches its theme tenderly and with romance. But amid all the romance Euripides cannot keep his hand from unveiling the weak spot in the sacred legend. Alcestis, no doubt, is beautiful, and it was beautiful of her to die. But what was it of Admetus to let her die? An ordinary playwright would elude the awkward question. Admetus would refuse his wife's sacrifice and she would perform it against his will or without his knowledge. We should somehow save our hero's character. Not so Euripides. His Admetus weeps tenderly over his wife, but he thinks it entirely suitable that she should die for him. The veil is not removed from his eyes till his old father, Pheres, who has bluntly refused to die for anybody, comes to bring offerings to Alcestis' funeral. A quarrel breaks out between the two selfish men, brilliantly written, subtle and merciless, in which Admetus's weakness is laid bare. The scene is a great grief to the purely romantic reader, but it just makes the play profound instead of superficial.

All the plays of 438 are, in different ways, typical of their author. And we will spend a little time on each. The Alcmaeon in Psôphis was what we should call a romance. Alcmaeon was the son of that Eriphyle who betrayed her husband to death for the sake of a charmed necklace which had once belonged to Harmonia, the daughter of Ares. Alcmaeon slew his mother and became in consequence mad and accursed. Seeking purification he fled to the land of Psôphis, where the King cleansed him and gave him the hand of his daughter Arsinoë, who duly received the necklace. However, Alcmaeon's sin was too great for any such cleansing. He wandered away, all the earth being accursed to him, till he should find some land that had not been in existence at the time of his sin and was consequently unpolluted. He discovered it in some alluvial islands, just then making their appearance at the mouth of the River Acheloüs. Here he at last found peace and married the daughter of Acheloüs, Callirrhoë. She asks for the necklace and Alcmaeon goes back to get it from Arsinoë. He professes to need it for his own purification and she willingly gives it him; then she finds that he really wants it for his new bride, and in fury has him murdered on his road home. A romantic and varied story with one fine touch of tragic passion.

The Telephus also deserves special mention. It had apparently the misfortune to be seen by Aristophanes, then a boy about sixteen. At any rate the comedian was never able to forget it, and we know it chiefly from his parodies. It struck out a new style in Attic drama, the style of adventure and plot-interest, which threw to the winds the traditional tragic dignities and pomps. The usual convention in tragedy was to clothe the characters in elaborate priestly dress with ritual masks carefully graduated according to the rank of the character. Such trappings came to Tragedy as an inheritance from its old magico-religious days, and it never quite succeeded in throwing them off, even in its most vital period. It is very difficult for us to form a clear notion what the ordinary Greek tragedy looked like in 438, and how much we should have noticed any great change of dressing in the Telephus. But there was a change which raised a storm of comment. Telephus was a King of Mysia, not very far from the Troad. The Greeks in sailing for Troy had missed their way and invaded Telephus' country by mistake. He had fought them with great effect but had been wounded by Achilles with his magic spear. The wound would not close, and an oracle told Telephus "the wounder shall heal." The Greeks were back in Greece by this time, planning a new invasion of Troy. The king goes, lame and disguised as a beggar, into the heart of the Greek army and into Agamemnon's palace. Euripides, since the king had to be a beggar, dressed him as a beggar, with rags and a wallet. It is hard to see how he could possibly have done otherwise, but we may surmise that his beggar's dress was a little more realistic and less merely symbolical than his audience expected. In any case, though critics were shocked, the practice established itself. Telephus and Philoctêtes were afterwards regularly allowed to dress in "rags," even in the work of Sophocles.

There were great scenes owing to the boldness of the ragged and intrusive stranger. The Greek chieftains proposed to kill him, but granted him at last the right of making one speech to save his life. He seems to have spoken beside, or over, the headsman's block. And the case he had to plead was characteristic of Euripides. The Greeks considered quite simply that Telephus was their enemy and must be destroyed on their next expedition. The beggar explained that Telephus had found his country ravaged and was bound to defend it. Every man among the Greeks would have done the same; there is nothing to blame Telephus for. At the end of this scene, apparently, the beggar was discovered. It is Telephus himself speaking! They fly to their spears. But Telephus has snatched up the baby prince, Orestes, from his cradle and stands at bay; if one of his enemies moves the child shall die. Eventually they accept his terms and make peace with him. A fine melodrama, one would guess, and a move in the direction of realism—a direction which Euripides only followed within certain strict limits. But we find two marks of Euripides the philosopher. The beggar who pleads for reasonable justice towards the national enemy strikes a note which Euripides himself often had to sound afterwards. It was not for nothing that Aristophanes in his Acharnians, thirteen years later, used a parody of this scene in order to plead the dangerous cause of reasonableness towards Sparta. The other mark is a curious tang of sadness at the close. The Greeks demand that Telephus, so brave and resourceful, shall be their ally against Troy. But his wife is a Trojan princess and he refuses. He consents reluctantly to show the army the road to his wife's fatherland and then turns away.

The remaining play of the trilogy performed in 438 strikes a chord that proved more dangerous to Euripides. The Cretan Women told the story of Aëropê, a Cretan princess who secretly loved a squire or young soldier. Her intrigue is discovered, and her father gives her to a Greek sailor to throw into the sea. The sailor spares her life and takes her to Greece. The story as it stands is a common ballad motive and not calculated to disturb any one. But the disciple of the sophists did not leave these romances where he found them. He liked to think them out in terms of real life. The songs in which Aëropê poured out her love were remembered against Euripides after his death. It was all very well to sympathize in a remote artistic way with these erring damsels; but Euripides seemed to come too near raising an actual doubt whether the damsel had done anything so very wrong at all, that respectable people should want to murder her. Euripides is, as a matter of fact, not loose but highly austere in his moral tone. But next to religion itself, the sphere of sexual conduct has always been the great field for irrational taboos and savage punishments, and the sophists naturally marked it as a battle-field. The kings of Egypt commonly married their sisters, and did so on religious grounds: to a Greek such marriage was an unspeakable sin. There is a problem here, and Euripides raised it sharply in a play, Aeolus, based on the old fairy-tale of the King of the winds who dwells as a patriarch on his floating island with his twelve sons married to his twelve daughters. "Canst face mine eyes, fresh from thy deed of shame?" says the angry father in this play; and his son answers, "What is shame, when the doer feels no shame?" Euripides also treated several times legends where a god became the lover of a mortal maiden, and, as we shall see in the Ion, he loved to rouse sympathy for the maiden and contempt for the god (p. 121). In one case he even treats, through a mist of strange religious mysticism, the impossible amour of Pasiphaë of Crete with the Cretan Bull-god. It is interesting, however, to observe that there is in Euripides no trace of sympathy for the one form of perverted indulgence on which the ancient tone was markedly different from ours. It is reserved for the bestial Cyclops and Laius the accursed.

Adventure, brilliance, invention, romance and scenic effect; these together with delightful lyrics, a wonderful command over the Greek language, and a somewhat daring admixture of sophistic wisdom which sometimes took away a spectator's breath, were probably the qualities which the ordinary public had felt in Euripides' work up to the year 438. They perhaps felt also that these pleasant gifts were apt to be needlessly marred by a certain unintelligible note of discord. It was a pity; and, as the man was now forty-six, he ought surely to have learnt how to smooth it out!

It was not smoothness that was coming.

CHAPTER IV

The next play of which we have full knowledge must have staggered its audience. The Medea was promptly put by the official judges at the bottom of the list of competing plays, and thereafter took its place, we do not know how soon, as one of the consummate achievements of the Greek tragic genius. Its stamp is fixed on all the imagination of antiquity.

The plot of the Medea begins where that of the Daughters of Pelias (p. 69) ended. Jason had fled with Medea and her two children to Corinth, which is ruled by Creon, an old king with a daughter but no son to succeed him. The famous warrior-prince will just suit Creon as a son-in-law, if only he will dismiss his discreditable barbarian mistress. Jason has never been able to tell the truth to Medea yet; who could? He secretly accepts Creon's terms; he marries the princess; and Creon descends on Medea with soldiers to remove her instantly from the territory of Corinth. Medea begs for one day in which to make ready for exile, for the children's sake. One day will be enough. By desperate flattery and pleading she gets it. There follows a first scene with Jason, in which man and woman empty their hearts on one another—at least they try to; but even yet some fragments of old habit and conventional courtesy prevent Jason from telling the full truth. Still it is a wonderful scene, Jason reasonable and cold, ready to recognize all her claims and provide her with everything she needs except his own heart's blood; Medea desolate and half mad, asking for nothing but the one thing he will not give. Love to her is the whole world, to him it is a stale memory. This scene ends in defiance, but there is another in which Medea feigns repentance and submission, and sends Jason with the two children to bear a costly gift to the new bride. It may, she suggests, induce Creon to spare the children and let her go to exile alone. The gift is really a robe of burning poison, which has come to Medea from her divine ancestor, the Sun. The bride dies in agony together with her father who tries to save her. Jason rushes to save his two children from the vengeance which is sure to come upon them from the kinsmen of the murdered bride; but Medea has already slain them with her own hand and stands laughing at him over their bodies. She too suffers, but she loves the pain, since it means that he shall have happiness no more. The Daughter of the Sun sails away on her dragon-chariot and an ecstasy of hate seems to blind the sky.

The Medea shows a new mastery of tragic technique, especially in the extraordinary value it gets out of the chorus (p. 240). But as illustrating the life of Euripides there are one or two special points in it that claim notice. In the first place it states the cause of a barbarian woman against a Greek man who has wronged her. Civilized men have loved and deserted savage women since the world began, and I doubt if ever the deserted one has found such words of fire as Medea speaks. The marvel is that in such white-hot passion there is room for satire. But there is; and even a reader can scarcely withhold a bitter laugh when Jason explains the advantage he has conferred on Medea by bringing her to a civilized country. But Medea is not only a barbarian; she is also a woman, and fights the horrible war that lies, an eternally latent possibility, between woman and man. Some of the most profound and wounding things said both by Medea and by Jason might almost be labelled in a book of extracts "Any wife to any husband," or "Any husband to any wife." And Medea is also a witch; she is also at heart a maniac. It is the madness produced by love rejected and justice denied, by the sense of helpless, intolerable wrong. A lesser poet might easily have made Medea a sympathetic character, and have pretended that long oppression makes angels of the oppressed. In the great chorus which hymns the rise of Woman to be a power in the world it would have been easy to make the Woman's day a day of peace and blessing. But Euripides, tragic to the heart and no dealer in pleasant make-believe, saw things otherwise; when these oppressed women strike back, he seems to say, when these despised and enslaved barbarians can endure no longer, it will not be justice that comes but the revenge of madmen.

This kind of theme was not in itself likely to please an audience; but what always galls the average theatre-goer most in a new work of genius is not the subject but the treatment. Euripides' treatment of his subject was calculated to irritate the plain man in two ways. First it was enigmatic. He did not label half his characters bad and half good; he let both sides state their case and seemed to enjoy leaving the hearer bewildered. And further, he made a point of studying closely and sympathetically many regions of thought and character which the plain man preferred not to think of at all. When Jason had to defend an obviously shabby case, no gentleman cared to hear him; but Euripides insisted on his speaking. He enjoyed tracking out the lines of thought and feeling which really actuate men, even fine men like Jason, in Jason's position. When Medea was revealed as obviously a wicked woman the plain man thought that such women should simply be thrashed, not listened to. But Euripides loved to trace all her complicated sense of injustice to its origins, and was determined to understand and to explain rather than to condemn. The plain man had a kind of justification for saying that Euripides actually seemed to like these traitors and wicked women; for such thorough understanding as this involves always a good deal of sympathy.

This charge could with even more reason be brought against another masterpiece of drama, which followed three years after the Medea. The Hippolytus (428 B.C.) did indeed win the first prize from the official judges, besides establishing itself in the admiration of after ages and inspiring Seneca and Racine to their finest work. But it profoundly shocked public opinion at the same time. The plot is a variant of a very old theme found in ancient Egypt and in the Pentateuch. Theseus, not here the ideal democrat on the Athenian throne, but the stormy and adventurous hero of the poets, had early in life conquered the Amazons and ravished their virgin Queen. She died, leaving a son like herself, Hippolytus. Theseus some twenty years after married Phaedra, the young daughter of Minos, king of Crete, and she by the evil will of Aphrodite fell in love with Hippolytus. She told no one her love, and was trying to starve herself to death, when her old Nurse contrived to worm the secret from her and treacherously, under an oath of secrecy, told it to Hippolytus. Phaedra, furious with the Nurse and with Hippolytus, in a blind rage of self-defence, writes a false accusation against Hippolytus and hangs herself. Hippolytus, charged by Theseus with the crime, will not break his oath and goes out to exile under his father's curse. The gods, in fulfilment of the curse, send death to him, but before he actually dies reveal his innocence. The story which might so easily be made ugly or sensual is treated by Euripides with a delicate and austere purity. In construction, too, and general beauty of workmanship, though not in greatness of idea or depth of passion, the Hippolytus is perhaps the finest of all his plays, and has still a great appeal on the stage. But the philistine was vaguely hurt and angered by the treatment, so tender and yet so inexorable, accorded to a guilty love, and doubtless the more conventional Athenian ladies shocked themselves over the bare idea of such a heroine being mentioned. It gives us some measure of the stupidity of public criticism at the time, that we find special attacks made upon one phrase of Hippolytus. In his first rage with the Nurse he vows he will tell Theseus of her proposal. She reminds him of his oath, and he cries:

"'Twas but my tongue, 'twas not my heart that swore."

It is a passing flash of indignation at the trap in which he has been caught. When the time comes he keeps his oath at the cost of his life. Yet the line is repeatedly cited as showing the dreadful doctrines of Euripides and the sophists; doctrines that would justify any perjury!

The Hippolytus, as we have it, is a rewritten play. In his first version Euripides had a scene in which Phaedra actually declared her love. This more obvious treatment was preferred by Seneca and Racine; but Euripides in his second thoughts reached a far more austere and beautiful effect. His Phaedra goes to her death without having spoken one word to Hippolytus: she has heard him but has not answered. The Hippolytus has more serene beauty than any of Euripides' plays since the Alcestis, and is specially remarkable as the first great drama on the subject of tragic or unhappy love, a theme which has been so extraordinarily fruitful on the modern stage. To contemporaries it was also interesting as one of the earliest treatments of a purely local Attic story, which had not quite found its way into the great sagas of epic tradition.

The note of the Medea was struck again some two years later (426?) in a play almost equally powerful and more horrible, the Hecuba. The heroine is the famous Queen of Troy, a barbarian woman like Medea, majestic and beautiful at the beginning of the action and afterwards transformed by intolerable wrongs into a kind of devil. Her "evils" are partly the ordinary evils that come to the conquered in war, but they are made worse by the callousness of her Greek conquerors. The play strikes many notes of special bitterness. For instance, the one champion whom Hecuba finds among her conquerors is the general, Agamemnon. He pleads her cause in the camp, because, God help him! he has taken her daughter Cassandra, the mad prophetess vowed to eternal virginity, to be his concubine, and consequently feels good-natured. There is another note, remarkable in an Athenian. The mob of the Greek army, in a frenzy of superstition, clamour to have a Trojan princess sacrificed at Achilles' tomb. In the debate on this subject we are told that several princes spoke; among them the two sons of Theseus, the legendary kings of Athens. They would surely, as enlightened Athenians, prevent such atrocities? On the contrary, all we hear is that they spoke against one another, but both were for the murder! At the end of the Hecuba, as at the end of the Medea, we are wrought to a pitch of excitement at which incredible legends begin to seem possible. History related that the Queen of Troy, maddened by her wrongs, had been transformed into a kind of Hell-hound with fiery eyes, whom sailors saw at night prowling round the hill where she was stoned. In her bloody revenge on the only enemy she can trap into her power, she seems already to have become this sort of being in her heart, and when her blind and dying victim prophesies the coming transformation, it seems natural. One only feels that perhaps the old miraculous stories are true after all. The one light that shines through the dark fury of the Hecuba is the lovely and gentle courage, almost the joy, with which the virgin martyr, Polyxena, goes to her death.

I have taken the Hecuba slightly before its due date, because of its return with increased bitterness to the tone and subject of the Medea. We will now go back. There had been in the interim a change in the poet's mind, or, at the least, a strong clash of conflicting emotions. The Medea was produced in 431, the first year of the Peloponnesian War. This war, between the Athenian empire, representing the democratic and progressive forces of Greece, and the Peloponnesian confederacy with Sparta at its head, lasted with one interruption for twenty-seven years and ended in the capture of Athens and the destruction of her power. When war was first declared it represented the policy of Pericles, the great statesman of the Enlightenment, the friend of Anaxagoras, and of those whom Euripides honoured most. It seemed at first like a final struggle between the forces of progress and those of resolute darkness. Pericles in a famous speech, which is recorded for us by Thucydides, had explained to his adherents the great causes for which Athens stood; had proclaimed her as the Princess of Cities for whom it was a privilege to die; and urged them, using a word more vivid in Greek than it is in English, to stand about her like a band of Lovers round an Immortal Mistress. Euripides was as a matter of fact still going through his military service and must have seen much hard fighting in these first years of the war.

He responded to Pericles' call by a burst of patriotic plays. Even in the Medea there is one chorus, a little out of place perhaps, but famous in after days, describing the glories of Athens. They are not at all the conventional glories attributed by all patriots to their respective countries. "It is an old and happy land which no conqueror has ever subdued; its children walk delicately through air that shines with sunlight; and Wisdom is the very bread that they eat." (The word is "sophia," embracing Wisdom, Knowledge, Art, Culture; there is no one word for it in English, and the names for the various parts of it have lost their poetry.) "A river," he continues, "flows through the land; and legend tells that Cypris, the Goddess of Love, has sailed upon it and dipped her hand in the water; and now when the river-wind at evening blows it comes laden with a spirit of longing; but it is not ordinary love, it is a Passion and a great Desire for all kinds of godlike endeavour, a Love that sits with Wisdom upon her throne." . . . "A pity the man should be so priggish." We may imagine the comment of the average Athenian paterfamilias.

Towards the beginning of the war we may safely date the Children of Heracles, a mutilated but beautiful piece, which rings with this particular spirit of patriotism (cf. p. 41 above). Heracles is dead; his children and mother are persecuted and threatened with death by his enemy, Eurystheus, king of Argos. Under the guidance of their father's old comrade, Iolaus, they have fled from Argos, and tried in vain to find protectors in every part of Greece. No city dares protect them against the power of Argos. At the opening of the play we find the children and Iolaus clinging as suppliants to an altar in Athens. The herald of Argos breaks in upon them, flings down the old man and prepares to drag the children off. "What hope can Iolaus possibly cherish?" Iolaus trusts in two things, in Zeus who will protect the innocent, and in Athens which is a free city and not afraid. The king of Athens, a son of Theseus, appears and rebukes the herald. The herald's argument is clear: "These children are Argive subjects and are no business of yours; further, they are utterly helpless and will be no possible good to you as allies. And if you do not give them up peacefully, Argos declares instant war." The king "wishes for peace with all men; but he will not offend God, nor betray the innocent; also he rules a free city and will take no orders from any outside power. As to the fate of these children not being his business, it is always the business of Athens to save the oppressed." One remembers the old claim, emphatically approved by the historian of the Persian Wars, that Athens was the saviour of Hellas. One remembers also the ultimatum of the Peloponnesian confederacy which Pericles rejected on the eve of the present war; and the repeated complaints of the Corinthians that Athens "will neither rest herself nor let others rest." These supply the clue to a large part of the patriotism of the Children of Heracles. There is another element also, and perhaps one that will better stand the test of impartial criticism, in Euripides' ideal of Athens. She will be true to Hellas and all that Hellas stands for: for law, for the gods of mercy, for the belief in right rather than force. Also, as the king of Athens is careful to observe, for democracy and constitutional government. He is no despot ruling barbarians.

The same motives recur with greater fulness and thoughtfulness in another play of the early war time—the exact year is not certain—the Suppliant Women. Scholars reading the play now, in cool blood, with the issues at stake forgotten, are inclined to smile at a sort of pedantry in the poet's enthusiasm. It reminds one of the punctiliousness with which Shelley sometimes gives one the sincere milk of the word according to Godwin. This play opens, like the last, with a scene of supplication. A band of women—Argive mothers they are this time, whose sons have been slain in war against Thebes—have come to Athens as suppliants. They are led by Adrastus, the great and conquered lord of Argos, and finding Aethra, the king's mother, at her prayers beside the altar, have surrounded her with a chain of suppliant branches which she dares not break. They only ask that Theseus, her son, shall get back for them the bodies of their dead sons, whom the Thebans, contrary to all Hellenic law, have flung out unburied for dogs to tear. Theseus at first refuses, on grounds of policy, and the broken-hearted women take up their branches and begin to go, when Aethra, who has been weeping silently, breaks out: "Is this kind of wrong to be allowed to exist?"

"Thou shalt not suffer it, thou being my child!
Thou hast seen men scorn thy City, call her wild
Of counsel, mad; thou hast seen the fire of morn
Flash from her eyes in answer to their scorn.
Come toil on toil; 'tis this that makes her grand;
Peril on peril! And common states, that stand
In caution, twilight cities, dimly wise—
Ye know them, for no light is in their eyes.
Go forth, my son, and help. My fears are fled.
Women in sorrow call thee, and men dead."
(Suppl. 320 ff.)

Theseus accepts his mother's charge. It has been his old habit to strike wherever he saw oppression without counting the risk; and it shall never be said of him that an ancient Law of God was set at naught when he and Athens had power to enforce it. It is Athens as the "saviour of Hellas" that we have here. It is Athens the champion of Hellenism and true piety, but it is also the Athens of free thought and the Enlightenment. For later on, when the dead bodies are recovered from the battle-field, they are a ghastly sight. The old unreflecting Greece would in the first place have thought them a pollution, a thing which only slaves must be sent to handle. In the second place, since the mothers were making lamentation, the bodies must be brought to their eyes, so as to improve the lamentation. But Theseus feels differently on both points. Why should the mothers' grief be made more bitter? Let the bodies be burned in peace and the decent ashes given to the mothers. And as to the defilement, the king himself, we hear, has taken up the disfigured bodies in his arms and washed their wounds and "shown them love." No slave touched them. "How dreadful! Was he not ashamed?" asks a bystander—the Greek word means something between "ashamed" and "disgusted." "No," is the answer: "Why should men be repelled by one another's sufferings?" (768) It is a far-reaching answer, with great consequences. It is the antique counterpart of St. Francis kissing the leper's sores. The man of the herd is revolted by the sight of great misery and inclines to despise and even hate the sufferer; the man of the enlightenment sees deeper, and the feeling of revulsion passes away in the wish to help.

We spoke of a slight pedantry in the enthusiasms of the Suppliant Women. It is illustrated even by points like this, and by a tendency in Theseus to lecture on good manners and the Athenian constitution. The rude Theban herald enters asking, "Who is monarch of this land?" using the word "tyrannos" for "monarch." Theseus corrects him at once. "There is no 'tyrannos' here. This is a free city; and when I say a free city, I mean one in which the whole people by turns takes part in the sovereignty, and the rich have no privilege as against the poor" (399-408). These dissertations on democratic government could stir men's passions and force their way into scenes of high poetry legitimately enough at a time when men were fighting and dying for their democracy. To those who are not "Lovers" of the beautiful city they will seem cold and irrelevant.

Other plays of this period show marks of the same great wave of love for Athens. The lost plays Aigeus, Theseus, Erechtheus, all on Attic subjects, can be dated in the first years of the war; the Hippolytus is built on an old legend of the Acropolis and a poetic love of Athens shines through the story. The Andromache especially is a curious document, the meaning of which is discussed later on (p. 112). But the two plays we have described at length, The Children of Heracles and the Suppliant Women, give the best idea of what patriotism meant to our poet. With most men patriotism is a matter of association and custom. They stick to their country because it is theirs; to their own habits and prejudices and even neighbours for the same reason. But with Euripides his ideals came before his actual surroundings. He loved Athens because Athens meant certain things, and if the real Athens should cease to mean those things he would cast her out of his heart. At least he would try to do so; in point of fact that is always a very difficult thing to do. But if ever Athens should be false, it was pretty certain that Euripides would find hatred mingling with his betrayed love. There were signs of this even in the Medea and the Hecuba.

But before dealing with that subject we must dwell for a few moments upon another fine play, which marks in more than one sense the end of a period. The Heracles, written about the year 423, shows Theseus in the same rôle of Athenian hero. In the Suppliant Women he had helped Adrastus and the Argive mothers and shown them the path of true Hellenism; in the Heracles he comes to the rescue of Heracles in his fall. That hero has been mad and slain his own children; he has recovered and awakes to find himself bound to a pillar, with dead bodies that he cannot recognize round about him. He rages to be set free. He compels those who know to tell him the whole truth. Frantic with shame and horror, he wishes to curse God and die, when he sees Theseus approaching. Theseus has been his friend in many hard days and Heracles dares not face him nor speak to him. The touch of one so blood-guilty, the sound of his voice, the sight of his face, would bring pollution. He shrouds himself in his mantle and silently waves Theseus away. In a moment his friend's arms are round him, and the shrouding mantle is drawn off. There is no such thing as pollution; no deed of man can stain the immortal sunlight, and a friend's love does not fear the infection of blood. Heracles is touched: he thanks Theseus and is now ready to die. God has tempted him too far, and he will defy God. Theseus reminds him of what he is: the helper of man, the powerful friend of the oppressed; the Heracles who dared all and endured all; and now, like a common, weak-hearted man, he speaks of suicide! "Hellas will not suffer you to die in your blindness!" (1254). The great adventurer is softened and won over by the "wisdom" of Theseus, and goes to Athens to fulfil, in spite of suffering, whatever further tasks life may have in store for him.

This condemnation of suicide was unusual in antiquity; and the Heracles also contains one remarkable denial of the current myths, the more remarkable because, as Dr. Verrall has pointed out, it seems almost to upset the plot of the play. Heracles' madness is sent upon him by the malignity of Hera; we see her supernatural emissary entering the room where Heracles lies. And the hero himself speaks of his supernatural adventures. Yet he also utters the lines:

Say not there be adulterers in Heaven
Nor prisoner gods and gaoler. Long ago
My heart has known it false and will not alter.
God, if he be God, lacketh naught. All these
Are dead unhappy tales of minstrelsy.
(Her. 1341; cf. Iph. Taur. 380-392; Bellerophon fr. 292.)

But in another way, too, the Heracles marks an epoch in the poet's life. It seems to have been written in or about the year 423, and it was in 424 that Euripides had reached the age of sixty and was set free from military service. He had had forty years of it, steady work for the most part; fighting against Boeotians, Spartans, Corinthians, against Thracian barbarians, in all probability also against other people further overseas. We have no record of the campaigns in which Euripides served; but we have by chance an inscription of the year 458, when he was twenty-six, giving the names of the members of one particular tribe, the Sons of Erechtheus, who fell in war in that one year. They had fallen "in Cyprus, in

Egypt, in Phoenicia, at Halieis, in Aegina and at Megara." There were ten such tribes in Athens. And this record gives some notion of the extraordinary energy and ubiquity of the Athenian armies.

It is strange to reflect on the gulf that lies between the life of an ancient poet and his modern descendants. Our poets and men of letters mostly live either by writing or by investments eked out by writing. They are professional writers and readers and, as a rule, nothing else. It is comparatively rare for any one of them to face daily dangers, to stand against men who mean to kill him and beside men for whom he is ready to die, to be kept a couple of days fasting, or even to work in the sweat of his body for the food he eats. If such things happen by accident to one of us we cherish them as priceless "copy," or we even go out of our way to compass the experience artificially.

But an ancient poet was living hard, working, thinking, fighting, suffering, through most of the years that we are writing about life. He took part in the political assembly, in the Council, in the jury-courts; he worked at his own farm or business; and every year he was liable to be sent on long military expeditions abroad or to be summoned at a day's notice to defend the frontier at home. It is out of a life like this, a life of crowded reality and work, that Aeschylus and Sophocles and Euripides found leisure to write their tragedies; one writing 90, one 127, and the third 92! Euripides was considered in antiquity a bookish poet. He had a library—in numbers probably not one book for every hundred that Tennyson or George Meredith had: he was a philosopher, he read to himself. But on what a background of personal experience his philosophy was builded! It is probably this immersion in the hard realities of life that gives ancient Greek literature some of its special characteristics. Its firm hold on sanity and common sense, for instance; its avoidance of sentimentality and paradox and various seductive kinds of folly; perhaps also its steady devotion to ideal forms and high conventions, and its aversion from anything that we should call "realism." A man everlastingly wrapped round in good books and safe living cries out for something harsh and real—for blood and swear-words and crude jagged sentences. A man who escapes with eagerness from a life of war and dirt and brutality and hardship to dwell just a short time among the Muses, naturally likes the Muses to be their very selves and not remind him of the mud he has just washed off. Euripides has two long descriptions of a battle, one in the Children of Heracles and one in the Suppliant Women; both are rhetorical Messenger's Speeches, conventionally well-written and without one touch that suggests personal experience. It is curious to compare these, the writings of the poet who had fought in scores of hand-to-hand battles, with the far more vivid rhapsodies of modern writers who have never so much as seen a man pointing a gun at them. Aeschylus indeed has written one splendid battle piece in the Persians. But even there there is no realism; it is the spirit of the war of liberation that thrills in us as we read, it is not the particular incidents of the battle.

Forty years of military service finished: as the men of sixty stepped out of the ranks they must have had a feeling of mixed relief and misgiving. They are now officially "Gerontes," Old Men: they are off hard work, and to be at the end of hard work is perilously near being at the end of life. There is in the Heracles a wistful chorus, put in the mouths of certain Theban elders (637 ff.), "Youth is what I love for ever; Old Age is a burden upon the head, a dimness of light in the eyes, heavier than the crags of Etna. Fame and the crown of the East and chambers piled with gold, what are they all compared with Youth?" A second life is what one longs for. To have it all again and live it fully; if a man has any aretê in him, any real life left in his heart, that is what ought to be possible. . . . For Euripides himself it seems there is still a life to be lived. The words are important and almost untranslatable. "I will never cease mingling together the Graces and the Muses"—such words are nearly nonsense, like most literal translations. The "Graces" or Charities are the spirits of fulfilled desire, the Muses are all the spirits of "Music" or of "Wisdom"—of History and Mathematics, by the way, just as much as Singing and Poetry. "I will not rest. I will make the spirits of Fulfilled Desire one with the spirits of Music, a marriage of blessedness. I care not to live if the Muses leave me; their garlands shall be about me for ever. Even yet the age-worn minstrel can turn Memory into song."

Memory, according to Greek legend, was the mother of the Muses; and the "memory" of which Euripides is thinking is that of the race, the saga of history and tradition, more than his own. The Muses taught him long ago their mystic dance, and he will be theirs for ever; he will never from weariness or faint heart ask them to rest. He was thinking doubtless of the lines of the old poet Alcman to his dancing maidens, lines almost the most beautiful ever sung by Greek lips: "No more, ye maidens honey-throated, voices of longing; my limbs will bear me no more. Would God I were a ceryl-bird, over the flower of the wave with the halcyons flying, and never a care in his heart, the sea-blue bird of the spring!" Euripides asks for no rest: cares and all, he accepts the service of the Muses and prays that he may bear their harness to the end. It was a bold prayer, and the Muses in granting it granted it at a heavy price.

CHAPTER V

LIFE CONTINUED: THE EMBITTERING OF THE WAR: ALCIBIADES AND THE DEMAGOGUES: THE "ION": THE "TROJAN WOMEN"

Our Greek historians, with Thucydides at their head, are practically unanimous in associating with the Peloponnesian War a progressive degradation and embitterment in Greek public life, and a reaction against the old dreams and ideals. We can measure the change by many slight but significant utterances.

When Herodotus records his opinion that in the Persian Wars the Athenians had been "the Saviours of Hellas" he has to preface the remark by a curious apology (VII. 139): "Here I am compelled by necessity to express an opinion which will be offensive to most of mankind, but I cannot refrain from putting it in the way which I believe to be true." He was writing at the beginning of the Peloponnesian War, and by that time Athens was not the Saviour but "the Tyrant City." Her "allies" had from time to time refused to serve or tried to secede from the alliance; and one by one she had reduced them to compulsory subjection. The "League" had become confessedly an "Empire."

Even Pericles, the great statesman of the good time, who had sought and achieved so many fine ends, had failed to build up a free League based on a representative elected body. The possibility of such a plan had hardly yet been conceived in the world, though a rudimentary system of international councils did in some places exist between neighbouring villages; and Pericles must not be personally blamed for an error, however fatal, which no one living knew how to avoid. But he realized at last in 430 B.C. what Athens had come to (Thuc. II. 63): "Do not imagine you are fighting about a simple issue, the subjection or independence of certain cities. You have an Empire to lose, and a danger to face from those who hate you for your empire. To resign it now would be impossible—if at this crisis some timid and inactive spirits are hankering after Righteousness even at that price! For by this time your empire has become a Despotism (Tyrannis), a thing which it is considered unjust to acquire, but which can never be safely surrendered."

The same thought is emphasized more brutally by Cleon (Thuc. III. 37):

"I have remarked again and again that a democracy cannot govern an empire, and never more clearly than now. . . . You do not realize that when you make a concession to the allies out of pity, or are led away by their specious pleading, you commit a weakness dangerous to yourselves without receiving any gratitude from them. Remember that your empire is a Despotism exercised over unwilling men who are always in conspiracy against you." "Do not be misled," he adds a little later, "by the three most deadly enemies of empire, pity and charm of words and the generosity of strength" (Thuc. III. 40).

So much for the ideals of chivalry and freedom and "Sophia": for I think the second of Cleon's "enemies" refers especially to the eloquent wisdom of the philosophers. And as for democracy we do not hear now that "the very name of it is beautiful": we hear that it is no principle on which to govern an empire. And later on we shall hear Alcibiades, an Athenian of democratic antecedents, saying at Sparta: "Of course all sensible men know what democracy is, and I better than most, from personal experience; but there is nothing new to be said about acknowledged insanity" (Thuc. VI. 89).

The ideals failed, and, if we are to believe our contemporary authors, the men failed too. Pericles, with all his errors, was a man of noble mind; he was pure in motive, lofty, a born ruler; he led his people towards "beauty and wisdom," and he wished it to be written on his grave that no Athenian had put on mourning through his act. Cleon, they all tell us, was a bellowing demagogue; violent, not over honest, unscrupulous, blundering; only resolute to fight for the demos of Athens till he dropped and to keep the poor from starving at whatever cost of blackmailing the rich and flaying the allied cities. And when he—by good luck, as Thucydides considers—was killed in battle, he was succeeded by Hyperbolus, a caricature of himself—as a pun of the comic poets' puts it, a "Cleon in hyperbole." This picture has been subjected to just criticism in many details, but it represents on the whole the united voice of our ancient witnesses.

One character only shines out in this period with a lurid light. Alcibiades, so far as one can understand him at all from our fragmentary and anecdotal records, must have been something like a Lord Byron on a grand scale, turned soldier and statesman instead of poet. His disastrous end and his betrayal of all political parties have probably affected his reputation unfairly. Violent and unprincipled as he certainly was, the peculiar dissolute caddishness implied in the anecdotes is probably a misrepresentation of the kind that arises so easily against a man who has no friends. It needs an effort to imagine what he looked like before he was found out. Of noble birth and a nephew of Pericles; famous for his good looks and his distinguished, if insolent, manners; a brilliant soldier, an ambitious and far-scheming politician; a pupil of the philosophers and an especially intimate friend of Socrates, capable both of rising to great ideas and of expounding them to the multitude; he was hailed by a large party as the destined saviour of Athens, and seems for a time at least to have made the same impression upon Euripides. Even in the Suppliant Women, peace-play as it is, Euripides congratulates Athens on possessing in Theseus "a general good and young," and critics have connected the phrase with the election of Alcibiades, at a very early age, to be General in the year 420. More significant perhaps is the curious case of the Andromache. The ancient argument tells us definitely that it was not produced in Athens. And we find from another source that it was produced by one Democrates or Timocrates. Now Euripides had a friend called Timocrates, who was an Argive; so it looks as if the play had been produced in Argos. This would be astonishing but by no means inexplicable. It was an old Athenian policy to check Sparta by organizing a philo-Athenian league in the Peloponnese itself (Ar. Knights, 465 ff.). The nucleus was to consist in three states, Argos, Elis and Mantinea, which had been visited by Themistocles just after the Persian wars and had set up democracies on the Athenian model. It was Alcibiades who eventually succeeded in organizing this league in 420, and it seems likely that the Andromache was sent to Argos for production in much the same spirit in which Pindar used to send his Chorus of Dancers with a new song to compliment some foreign king. The play seems to contain a reference to the Peloponnesian War (734), it indulges in curiously direct denunciations of the Spartans (445 ff., 595 ff.), and the Spartan Menelaus is the villain of the piece—a more stagey villain than Euripides in his better moments would have permitted. We have also one doubtful external record of our poet's temporary faith in Alcibiades. In the year 420 there fell an observance of the Olympian Festival, the greatest of all the Pan-Hellenic Games, which carried with it a religious truce. Alcibiades succeeded in getting Sparta convicted of a violation of this truce, and consequently excluded from the Festival, which was a marked blow at her prestige. Then, entering himself as a competitor, he won with his own horses a whole series of prizes, including the first, in the four-horse chariot competition. And Plutarch, in his Life of Alcibiades, refers to a Victory Ode which was written for him on this occasion, "as report goes, by the poet Euripides" (ch. 11). This revival of the Pindaric Epinikion for a personal victory would fit in with the known character of Alcibiades; and it would be a sharp example of the irony of history if Euripides consented to write the Ode.

Euripides' delusion was natural and it was short-lived. The Suppliant Women points towards peace, and the true policy of Alcibiades was to make peace impossible. And even apart from that the ideals of the two men were antipathetic. The matter is summed up in the Frogs of Aristophanes, produced in 405, when the only question remaining about Alcibiades was whether he was more dangerous to the city as an honoured leader or as an enemy and exile. The two great poets of the Dead are asked for their advice on this particular subject and their answers are clear. Aeschylus says: "Submit to the lion's whelp;" Euripides rejects him with three scathing lines (Frogs, 1427 ff., cf. 1446 ff.). Long before the date of the Frogs Alcibiades had probably grown to be in the mind of Euripides the very type and symbol of the evil times.

All Greece—we have the emphatic and disinterested testimony of Thucydides for the statement—was gradually corrupted and embittered by the long war. Probably all war, as it accustoms people more and more to desperate needs and desperate expedients for meeting them, and sets more and more aside the common generosities and humanities of life, tends to some degradation of character. But this particular war was specially harmful. For one thing it was a struggle not simply between two foreign powers, but between two principles, oligarchy and democracy. In almost all the cities of the Athenian alliance there were large numbers of malcontent rich, who were only too ready, if chance offered, to overthrow the constitution, massacre the mob, and revolt to Sparta. In a good many of the cities on the other side there were masses of discontented poor who had been touched by the breath of democratic doctrines, and were anxious for a chance to cut the throats of the ruling Few. It was like the state of things produced in many cities of Europe by the French Revolution. A secret civil strife lay in the background behind the open war; and the open war itself was a long protracted struggle for life or death. Probably the most high-minded man when engaged in a death-grapple fights in much the same way as the most low-minded. And there can be no doubt that as the toils of war closed tighter round Athens, and she began to feel herself fighting, gasp by gasp, for both her empire and her life, the ideals of the Saviour of Hellas fell away from her. She fought with every weapon that came.

Such times called forth naturally the men that suited them. The assembly cared less to listen to decent and thoughtful people, not to speak of philosophers. It was feeling bitter and fierce and frightened and it liked speakers who were feeling the same. The same fear that made it cruel made it also superstitious. On one occasion the whole city went mad with alarm because of a prank played on some ancient figures of Hermes. On another a great army was lost because it and its general were afraid to move during an eclipse of the moon. So soon had Anaxagoras been forgotten.

Is this the result, one is inclined to ask, of the great ideals of democracy and enlightenment? Of course the old Tory type of Greek historian, like Mitford, revelled in an affirmative answer. But a more reflective view of history suggests a different explanation. We must distinguish carefully between the two notions, Enlightenment and Democracy. They happen to have gone together in two or three of the greatest periods of human progress and we are apt to regard them as somehow necessarily allied. But they are not. Doubtless Democracy is itself an exalted conception and belongs naturally to the ideas of the Enlightenment, just as does the belief in Reason, in the free pursuit of knowledge, in justice to the weak, the wish to be right rather than to be victorious, or the hatred of violence and superstition as such. But the trouble is that, in a backward and untrained people, the victory of democracy may result in the defeat of the other exalted ideas. The Athenian democracy as conceived by Pericles, Euripides or Protagoras was a free people, highly civilized and pursuing "wisdom," free from superstition and oppression themselves and helping always to emancipate others. But the actual rustics and workmen who voted for Pericles had been only touched on the surface by the "wisdom" of the sophists. They liked him because he made them great and admired and proud of being Athenians. But one must suspect that, when they were back at their farms and the spell of Pericles' "wisdom" was removed, they practised again the silliest and cruellest old agricultural magic, were terrified by the old superstitions, beat their slaves and wives and hated the "strangers" a few miles off, just as their grandfathers had done in the old times. What seems to have happened at the end of the war-time is that, owing largely to the democratic enthusiasm of the sophistic movement in Athens, the common people is strongly in power; owing to the same movement its old taboos and rules of conduct are a little shaken and less able to stand against strong temptation; but meantime the true moral lessons of the enlightenment, the hardest of all lessons for man to learn, have never worked into their bones. Just as the French Revolution called into power the brutal and superstitious peasant who was the product of the Old Régime and could never rise to the ideas of the Revolution, so the Athenian enlightenment had put into power the old unregenerate mass of sentiment that had not been permeated by the enlightenment. Cleon was no friend of sophists, but their avowed enemy. And when he told the Assembly in its difficulties simply to double the tribute of the allies and sack their towns if they did not pay; when he urged the killing in cold blood of all the Mitylenean prisoners, he was preaching doctrines that would probably have seemed natural enough in the old days, before any sophists had troubled men's minds with talk about duties towards dirty foreigners. And the people who followed his lead were the same sort of people who would naturally be terrified about the mutilation of a taboo image or an eclipse of the divine moon. What they had, perhaps, acquired from the sophistic movement was a touch of effrontery. Boeotians or Acarnanians might commit crimes, when they needed to, by instinct, without stating their reasons: in Athens you had at least to discuss the principle of the proposed crime and accept it for what it was worth. A cynic or a hypocrite trained in a sophistic school might offer occasional help with the theory.

Perhaps the earliest touch of Euripides' bitterness against his country comes, as we have seen, in the Hecuba (p. 89). But the period we have just reached, soon after the Heracles, is marked by one of the most ironic and enigmatical plays he ever wrote. The Ion is interesting in every line and contains one scene which is sometimes considered the most poignant in all Greek tragedy, yet it leaves every reader unsatisfied. Is it a pious offering to Apollo, the ancestor of the Ionian race? If so, why is Apollo the villain of the piece? Is it a glorification of ancient Athens, her legends and her shrines? If so, why are the shrines polluted by lustful gods, the legends made specially barbaric, and the beautiful earth-born Princess shown as a seduced woman and a would-be murderess? Nay, further, why does the hero of the play explain in a careful speech that he would sooner live a friendless slave in the temple at Delphi than a free man and a prince in such a place as Athens—a city "full of terror," where men "who are good and might show wisdom are silent and never come forward," while the men in power watch enviously round to destroy any possible rival? (598 ff. Cf. Euripides' words in Frogs, 1446 ff.) In Delphi he has peace, and is not jostled off the pavement by the scum of the earth (635)—a complaint which is often made in Greek literature about democratic Athens.

I think the best way to understand the Ion is to suppose that Euripides, in his usual manner, is just taking an old canonical legend, seeing the human drama and romance in it, and working it together in his own clear ironic mind till at last he throws out his play, saying: "There are your gods and your holy legends; see how you like them!" The irony is lurking at every corner, though of course the drama and romance come first.

The Ion is, of all the extant plays, the most definitely blasphemous against the traditional gods. Greek legend was full of stories of heroes born of the love of a god and a mortal woman. Such stories could be turned into high religious mysteries, as by Aeschylus in his Suppliant Women; into tender and reverent legends, as by Pindar in one or two odes. Euripides uses no such idealization. In play after play, Auge, Melanippe, Danae, Alope, he seems to have scarified such gods, as he does now in the Ion. Legend told that Ion, the hero-ancestor of the Ionians, was the son of the Athenian princess Creusa. Creusa was married to one Xuthus, an Aeolian soldier, but the real father of Ion was the god Apollo. Euripides treats the story as if Apollo were just a lawless ravisher, utterly selfish and ready to lie when pressed, though good-natured in his way when he lost nothing by it—a sort of Alcibiades, in fact. Xuthus is a butt; a foreigner with abrupt and violent manners, lied to by Apollo, befooled by his wife, disobeyed by her maids, and eventually made happy by the belief that her illegitimate son is really his own. Creusa herself, though drawn with extraordinary sympathy and beauty, is at heart a savage.

Creusa, when she bore her child, laid him, in her terror, in the same cavern where Apollo had ravished her: surely the god would save his own son. She came again and the child was gone. As a matter of fact the god had carried him in his cradle to Delphi, where he was discovered by the priestess and reared as a foundling in the temple courts. Creusa was then married to Xuthus, who knew nothing of her adventure. Some seventeen years or so afterwards, since the pair had no children, they came to Delphi to consult the god. Creusa there meets the foundling, Ion, and the two are strangely attracted to one another. She almost confides to him her story, and he tells her what he knows of his own. Meantime Xuthus goes in to ask the god for a child; the god tells him that the first person he meets on leaving the shrine will be his son. (This, of course, is a lie.) He meets Ion, salutes him as his son and embraces him wildly. The boy protests: "Do not," cries Xuthus, "fly from what you should love best on earth!" "I do not love teaching manners to demented foreigners," retorts the youth. Sobered by this, Xuthus tries, with Ion's help, to think out what the god can mean by saying that this youth is his son. His married life has always been correct; but once when he was a young man, there was a time . . . It was a great religious feast at Delphi and he was drunk. Ion accepts the explanation, though he evidently does not much like his new father. He makes difficulties about going to Athens. He is sorry for Creusa. He wishes to stay as he is. Xuthus decides that Creusa must be deceived; he will say he has taken a fancy to Ion and wishes to adopt him. Meantime let them have a great birth-feast . . . and if any of the Chorus say a word to Creusa they shall be hanged! Creusa enters, accompanied by one of Euripides' characteristic Old Slaves. The man has tended Creusa from childhood, lives for her and thinks of nothing else; he is utterly without scruple apart from her. The Chorus immediately tell Creusa what they know of the story. Ion is Xuthus's illegitimate son; he must have known it all the time; he has now, with the god's connivance, arranged to take the son back to Athens; as for Creusa, the god says she shall have no child. Stung to fury to think that her child is dead, that the boy whom she so loved is deliberately deceiving her, and that Apollo is adding this deliberate insult to his old brutal wrong, Creusa casts away shame and standing up in front of the great Temple cries out her reproach against the god. She is disgraced publicly and for ever, but at least she will drag down this devil who sits crowned and singing to the lyre while the women he has ravished go mad with grief and his babes are torn by wild beasts. In the horror-stricken silence that follows there is none to advise Creusa except the old Slave. Blindly devoted and fostering all her passions, he wrings from her line by line the detailed story of her seduction, and then calls for revenge. "Burn down the god's temple!" She dare not. "Poison Xuthus!" No; he was good to her when she was miserable. "Kill the bastard!" . . . Yes: she will do that. . . . The Slave takes poison with him and goes to poison Ion at the birth-feast. The plot fails; the Slave is taken and Creusa, pursued by the angry youth, flies to the altar. It is fury against fury, each bewildered to find such evil in the other, after their curious mutual attraction. Here the Delphian Prophetess enters, bringing with her the tokens that were with the foundling when she first came upon him in the temple courts. Creusa, amazed, recognizes the old basket-cradle in which she had exposed her own child.

She leaves the altar and gives herself up to Ion. For a moment it seems as if he would kill her; but he tests her story. What else is there in the basket? She names the things, her own shawl with gorgons on it, her own snake-twined necklace and wreath of undying olive. The mother confesses to the son and the son forgives her. But Apollo? What of him? He has lied. . . . Ion, temple-child as he is, is roused to rebellion: he will break through the screen of the sanctuary and demand of the god one plain answer—when he is stopped by a vision of Athena. She comes instead of Apollo, who fears to face the mortals he has wronged; she bids them be content and seek no further. Creusa forgives the god; Ion remains moodily silent.

The Ion is so rich in romantic invention that it sometimes seems to a modern reader curiously old-fashioned; it is full of motives—lost children, and strawberry-marks, and the cry of the mother's heart, and obvious double meanings—which have been repeated by so many plays since that we instinctively regard them as "out of date." It is redeemed by its passion and its sincere psychology. On the other hand, it is more ironical than any other extant Greek play. The irony touches every part of the story, excepting the actual tragedy of the wronged woman and the charming carelessness of the foundling's life. We should remember that an attack on the god of Delphi was not particularly objectionable in Athens. For that god, by the mouth of his official prophets, at the beginning of the war, had assured the Spartans that if they fought well they would conquer and that He, the God, would be fighting for them. The best that a pious Athenian could do for such a god as that was to suppose that the official prophets were liars. Still Euripides attacks much more than Delphi. If his thoughts ever strike home, it is not merely Delphi that will fall, it is the whole structure of Greek ritual and mythology. It is against the gods and against Athens that his irony cuts sharpest.

Irony is the mood of one who has some strong emotion within but will not quite trust himself on the flood of it. And romance is largely the mood of one turning away from realities that disgust him. In the year 416 B.C. Euripides, in his relation to Athens, was shaken for the first time out of any thought of either romance or irony. During the summer and winter of that year there occurred an event of very small military importance and no direct political consequences, to which nevertheless Thucydides devotes twenty-six continuous chapters in a very significant part of his work, the part just before the final catastrophe. The event is the siege and capture by the Athenians of a little island called Melos, the massacre of all its adult men and the enslavement of the women and children. The island had no military power. It had little commerce and lived on its own poor agriculture. Its population was not large: when it was depopulated five hundred colonists were enough to people it again. Why then this large place in Thucydides' brief and severe narrative? Only, I think, because of the moral issue involved and the naked clarity of the crime. Thucydides tells us of a long debate between the Athenian envoys and the Melian Council and professes to report the arguments used on each side. No doubt there is conscious artistic composition in the reports. We cannot conclude that any Athenian envoy used exactly these horrible words. But we can be sure that Thucydides took the war on Melos as the great typical example of the principles on which the Athenian war party were led to act in the later part of the war; we can go further and be almost sure that he selected it as a type of sin leading to punishment—that sin of "Hubris" or Pride which according to Greek ideas was associated with some heaven-sent blindness and pointed straight to a fall.

In cool and measured language the Athenian envoys explain to the Melian Senate—for the populace is carefully excluded—that it suits their purpose that Melos should become subject to their empire. They will not pretend—being sensible men and talking to sensible men—that the Melians have done them any wrong or that they have any lawful claim to Melos, but they do not wish any islands to remain independent: it is a bad example to the others. The power of Athens is practically irresistible: Melos is free to submit or to be destroyed. The Melians, in language carefully controlled but vibrating with suppressed bitterness, answer as best they can. Is it quite safe for Athens to break all laws of right? Empires are mortal; and the vengeance of mankind upon such a tyranny as this . . . ? "We take the risk of that," answer the Athenians; "the immediate question is whether you prefer to live or die." The Melians plead to remain neutral; the plea is, of course, refused. At any rate they will not submit. They know Athens is vastly stronger in men and ships and military skill; still the gods may help the innocent ("That risk causes us no uneasiness," say the envoys: "we are quite as pious as you"); the Lacedaemonians are bound by every tie of honour and kinship to intervene ("We shall of course see that they do not"); in any case we choose to fight and hope rather than to accept slavery. "A very regrettable misjudgement," say the Athenians; and the war proceeds to its hideous end.

As I read this Melian Dialogue, as it is called, again and again, I feel more clearly the note of deep and angry satire. Probably the Athenian war-party would indignantly have repudiated the reasoning put into the mouths of their leaders. After all they were a democracy; and, as Thucydides fully recognizes, a great mass of men, if it does commit infamies, likes first to be drugged and stimulated with lies: it seldom, like the wicked man in Aristotle's Ethics, "calmly sins." But in any case the massacre of Melos produced on the minds of men like Thucydides and Euripides—and we might probably add almost all the great writers who were anywise touched by the philosophic spirit—this peculiar impression. It seemed like a revelation of naked and triumphant sin. And we can not but feel the intention with which Thucydides continues his story. "They put to death all the Melians whom they found of man's estate, and made slaves of the women and children. And they sent later five hundred colonists and took the land for their own.

"And the same winter the Athenians sought to sail with a greater fleet than ever before and conquer Sicily. . . ." This was the great Sicilian expedition that brought Athens to her doom.

Euripides must have been brooding on the crime of Melos during the autumn and winter. In the spring, when the great fleet was still getting ready to sail, he produced a strange play, the work rather of a prophet than a mere artist, which was reckoned in antiquity as one of his masterpieces but which set a flame of discord for ever between himself and his people. One would like to know what Archon accepted that play and what rich man gave the chorus. It was called The Trojan Women, and it tells of the proudest conquest wrought by Greek arms in legend, the taking of Troy by the armies of Agamemnon. But it tells the old legend in a peculiar way. Slowly, reflectively, with little stir of the blood, we are made to look at the great glory, until we see not glory at all but shame and blindness and a world swallowed up in night. At the very beginning we see gods brooding over the wreck of Troy; as they might be brooding over that wrecked island in the Aegean, whose walls were almost as ancient as Troy's own.

It is from the Aegean that Poseidon has risen to look upon the city that is now a smoking ruin, sacked by the Greeks. "The shrines are empty and the sanctuaries run red with blood." The unburied corpses lie polluting the air; and the conquering soldiers, home-sick and uneasy, they know not why, roam to and fro waiting for a wind that will take them away from the country they have made horrible. Such is the handiwork of Athena, daughter of Zeus!

The name gives one a moment of shock. Athena is so confessedly the tutelary goddess of Athens. But Euripides was only following the regular Homeric story, in which Athena had been the great enemy of Troy, and the unscrupulous friend of the Greeks. Her name is no sooner mentioned than she appears. But she is changed. Her favourites have gone too far; they have committed "Hubris," insulted the altars of the gods and defiled virgins in holy places. Athena herself is now turned against her people. Their great fleet, flushed with conquest and stained with sin, is just about to set sail: Athena has asked Zeus the Father for vengeance against it, and Zeus has given it into her hand. She and Poseidon swear alliance; the storm shall break as soon as the fleet sets sail, and the hungry rocks of the Aegean be glutted with wrecked ships and dying men (95 ff.).

How are ye blind
Ye treaders down of Cities; ye that cast
Temples to desolation and lay waste
Tombs, the untrodden sanctuaries where lie
The ancient dead, yourselves so soon to die!

And the angry presences vanish into the night. Were the consciences of the sackers of Melos quite easy during that prologue?

Then the day dawns and the play begins, and we see what, in plain words, the great glory has amounted to. We see the shattered walls and some poor temporary huts where once was a city; and presently we see a human figure rising wearily from sleep. It is an old woman, very tired, her head and her back aching from the night on the hard ground. The old woman is Hecuba, lately the queen of Troy, and in the huts hard by are other captives, "High women chosen from the waste of war" to be slaves to the Greek chieftains. They are to be allotted this morning. She calls them and they come startled out of sleep, some terrified, some quiet, some still dreaming, one suddenly frantic. Through the rest of the play we hear bit by bit the decisions of the Greek army-council. Cassandra, the virgin priestess, is to be Agamemnon's concubine. The stupid and good-natured Herald who brings the news thinks it good news. How lucky for the poor helpless girl! And the King, too! There is no accounting for tastes; but he thinks it was that air of unearthly holiness in Cassandra which made Agamemnon fancy her. The other women are horror-stricken, but Cassandra is happy. God is leading her; her flesh seems no longer to be part of her; she has seen something of the mind of God and knows that the fate of Troy and of dead Hector is better than that of their conquerors. She sees in the end that she must discrown herself, take off the bands of the priestess and accept her desecration; she sees to what end she is fated to lead Agamemnon, sees the vision of his murdered body—murdered by his wife—cast out in precipitous places on a night of storm; and beside him on the wet rocks there is some one else, dead, outcast, naked . . . who is it? She sees it is herself, and goes forth to what is appointed (445 ff.).

The central portion of the play deals with the decision of the Greeks about Hector's little boy, Astyanax. He is only a child now; but of course he will grow, and he will form the natural rallying point for all the fugitive Trojans and the remnants of the great Trojan Alliance. On the principles of the Melian dialogue he is best out of the way. The Herald is sent to take the child from his mother, Andromache, and throw him over the battlements. He comes when the two women, Andromache and Hecuba, are talking together and the child playing somewhere near. Andromache has been allotted as slave to Pyrrhus, the son of Achilles, and is consulting with Hecuba about the horror she has to face. Shall she simply resist to the end, in the hope that Pyrrhus may hate and kill her, or shall she try, as she always has tried, to make the best of things? Hecuba advises: "Think of the boy and think of your own gentle nature. You are made to love and not to hate; when things were happy you made them happier; when they are miserable you will tend to heal them and make them less sore. You may even win Pyrrhus to be kind to your child, Hector's child; and he may grow to be a help to all who have once loved us. . . ." As they speak the shadow of the entering Herald falls across them; he cannot speak at first, but he has come to take the child to its death, and his message has to be given. This scene, with the parting between Andromache and the child which follows, seems to me perhaps the most absolutely heart-rending in all the tragic literature of the world. After rising from it one understands Aristotle's judgment of Euripides as "the most tragic of the poets."

For sheer beauty of writing, for a kind of gorgeous dignity that at times reminds one of Aeschylus and yet is compatible with the subtlest clashes of mood and character, the Trojan Women stands perhaps first among all the works of Euripides. But that is not its most remarkable quality. The action works up first to a great empty scene where the child's body is brought back to his grandmother, Hecuba, for the funeral rites. A solitary old woman with a dead child in her arms; that, on the human side, is the result of these deeds of glory. Then, in the finale, come scenes of almost mystical tone, in which Hecuba appeals first to the gods, who care nothing; then to the human dead who did at least care and love; but the dead, too, are deaf like the gods and cannot help or heed. Out of the noise and shame of battle there has come Death the most Holy and taken them to his peace. No friend among the dead, no help in God, no illusion anywhere, Hecuba faces That Which Is and finds somewhere, in the very intensity of Troy's affliction, a splendour which cannot die. She has reached in some sense not the bottom, but the crowning peak of her fortunes. Troy has already been set on fire by the Greeks in preparation for their departure, and the Queen rushes to throw herself into the flames. She is hurled back by the guards, and the women watch the flaming city till with a crash the great tower falls. The Greek trumpet sounds through the darkness. It is the sign for the women to start for their ships; and forth they go, cheated of every palliative, cheated even of death, to the new life of slavery. But they have seen in their very nakedness that there is something in life which neither slavery nor death can touch.

The play is a picture of the inner side of a great conquest, a thing which then, even more than now, formed probably the very heart of the dreams of the average unregenerate man. It is a thing that seemed beforehand to be a great joy, and is in reality a great misery. It is conquest seen when the heat of battle is over, and nothing remains but to wait and think; conquest not embodied in those who achieved it—we have but one glimpse of the Greek conquerors, and that shows a man contemptible and unhappy—but in those who have experienced it most fully, the conquered women.

We have so far treated the Trojan Women as though it stood alone. In reality of course it belonged to a group, and one cannot but ask what the other plays were, and whether their themes were such as could stand beside this and not be shrivelled into commonplace or triviality. Fortunately, though the plays are both lost, we know something about them. They were Palamedes and Alexander; and both are on great subjects. The Palamedes tells of the righteous man condemned by an evil world; the Alexander has for its hero a slave.

Slavery had always been one of the subjects that haunted Euripides. We do not happen to find in our remains of his work any definite pronouncement that slavery is "contrary to nature," as was held by most Greek philosophers of the succeeding century. Probably no practical man of the time could imagine a large industrial city living without the institution of slavery. But it is clear that Euripides hates it. It corrupts a man; it makes the slave cowardly and untrustworthy. Yet "many slaves are better men than their masters"; "many so-called free men are slaves at heart." And again, in the style of a Stoic, "A man without fear cannot be a slave" (fr. 958: cf. fr. 86, 511, etc.). Much more important than such statements as these, which are, according to his manner, generally put in the mouth of a slave, are the many instances of "sympathetic" and courageous slaves, and the panegyrics on men who have no slaves but work with their own hands. These show the bent of the poet's mind. It is not, however, till the year of the Trojan Women that he takes the bold step of actually making a slave his hero and filling his play with discussions of slavery, including a definite contest in aretê between the slaves and the masters. True, the slave turns out in the end to be a prince. The herdsman whose favourite bull the young nobles have seized for a sacrifice, and who pursues and challenges and eventually conquers them in strength and skill as well as magnanimity, turns out to be Alexander, son of Priam, who has been reared by the slave herdsmen of Mt. Ida. By our standards that is a pity. We should have preferred him a real slave. But probably on the Greek stage thus much of romance was inevitable, and after all it had its connection with real life. Many a Scythian and Thracian and even Phrygian chief, like this Alexander, must have stood for sale in Greek slave markets.

The root idea of the Palamedes, the righteous man falsely slain, has a momentous place in the history of Greek thought. It starts, of course, as a bitterness or a paradox. Righteousness to the fifth century Athenian was almost identical with social service, and, in a healthy society with normal conditions, the man who serves his city well will naturally be honoured by his city. But then comes the thought, itself fraught with the wisdom of the sophists: "What if the multitude is bent on evil, or is blind? There are many men who are evil but seem righteous; what if the man who is righteous seems to be evil?" Hence come the story of Aias in Pindar, and Palamedes in this play, and the ideal Righteous Man of Plato's Republic who "shall be scourged, tortured, bound . . . and at last impaled or crucified" (Rep. p. 362a). The idea runs through the various developments of later Greek mysticism and attains its culminating point in Christianity. It is in full concord with the tone of the Trojan Women.

We know little of the Palamedes. That hero was the true wise man, and his enemy was Odysseus, the evil man who "seemed wise" and had the ear of the multitude. Palamedes is falsely accused of treason, condemned by the unanimous voice of his judges and sent to death. Fragments tell us of some friend, perhaps a prisoner, carving message after message upon oar-blades and throwing them into the sea that the truth might be known; and we have two beautiful untranslatable lines uttered by the Chorus: "Ye have slain, ye Greeks, ye have slain the nightingale; the wingèd-one of the Muses who sought no man's pain." Tradition saw in the words a reference to the wise Protagoras, lately slandered to his death.

The consideration of these other plays of the same trilogy strengthens the impression that I receive already from the Trojan Women, an impression of some deepening of experience, some profound change that has worked into the writer's soul. Other critics, and notably Wilamowitz and Mr. Glover, have similarly felt that this play marks a turning point. It was not a change of front; it was not sudden; it was not dependent on visions or supernatural messages. It was the completion of a long process of strong feeling and intense thought, not the less sane because of its decided element of mysticism. It probably differed in many ways from the sudden and conscious conversions which began the ministry of certain Greek philosophers, both Cynic and Stoic, in the fourth and third centuries before Christ. It differed still more from the experience of Paul on the road to Damascus or Augustine beneath the fig-tree. But it does seem to me that in this tragedy the author shows a greatly increased sense of some reality that is behind appearances, some loyalty higher than the claims of friends or country, which supersedes as both false and inadequate the current moral code and the current theologies.

CHAPTER VI

AFTER THE "TROJAN WOMEN": EURIPIDES' LAST YEARS IN ATHENS: FROM THE "IPHIGENIA" TO THE "ORESTES"

Critics have used various words to describe the change of mood which followed the Trojan Women. They speak of a period of despair, pessimism, progressive bitterness, Verzweiflung und Weltschmertz. But such phrases seem to me misleading. In the first place I do not think they describe quite truly even the particular plays they are meant to describe; in the second, they do not allow for the great variety which subsists in the plays of this period. The mood of the Trojan Women is not exactly pessimism or despair; and whatever it is, it does not colour all the subsequent plays.

The plays after 415 fall into two main divisions. First the works of pure fancy or romance, in which the poet seems to turn intentionally away from reality. Such are the Iphigenîa in Tauris, the Helena and the Andromeda; they move among far seas and strange adventures and they have happy endings. Next there are the true tragedies, close to life, ruthlessly probing the depths of human nature; not more acutely bitter than such earlier works as the Medea and Hecuba, but with a bitterness more profound because it is comparatively free from indignation. The glory has fallen away and the burning anger with it. The poor miserable heroes and heroines . . . what else can you expect of them? Rage is no good; punishment worse than useless. The road to healing lies elsewhere.

A good key to the first of these types of play is to be seen in Aristophanes' comedy, The Birds. The gayest, sweetest and most irresponsible of all his plays, it was written just after the news of the final disaster in Sicily, when ruin stared Athens in the face. And the two heroes of it, disgusted with the ways of man, depart to live among the birds and build, with their help, a splendid Cloud City. In much the same spirit Euripides must have written his Andromeda. He produced it in 412, the same year in which he was invited by the anti-war government which came into power after the news of the great disaster to write the national epitaph on the soldiers slain in Sicily. He wrote the epitaph in the old severe untranslatable style of Simonides: "These men won eight victories over the Syracusans when the hand of God lay even between both." In English it seems cold; it seems hardly poetry. But in Greek it is like carved marble. Then, one must imagine, he turned right away from the present and spent his days with Andromeda. Only a few fragments of the Andromeda remain, but they are curiously beautiful; and the play as a whole seems to have been the one unclouded love-romance that Euripides ever wrote. It was fantastic, remote from life, with its heroine chained to a cliff over the blue sea awaiting the approach of the sea-monster, and its hero, Perseus, on winged sandals, appearing through the air to save her. Yet the fragments have a wistful ring: "O holy Night, how long is the path of thy chariot!" "By the Mercy that dwelleth in the sea caves, cease, O Echo; let me weep my fill in peace." Or the strange lines (fr. 135):

Methinks it is the morrow, day by day,
That cows us, and the coming thing alway
Greater than things to-day or yesterday.

There was a story told, in later times, of a tragedy-fever that fell on the folk of Abdêra, in Thrace, through this play, till in every street you could see young men walking as though in a dream, and murmuring to themselves the speech beginning, "O Love, high monarch over gods and men. . . ." The Andromeda was five hundred years old when people told that story.

The Iphigenîa in Tauris came one year earlier. It is one of the most beautiful of the extant plays, not really a tragedy in our sense nor yet merely a romance. It begins in gloom and rises to a sense of peril, to swift and dangerous adventure, to joyful escape. So far it is like romance. But it is tragic in the sincerity of the character-drawing. Iphigenîa, especially, with her mixed longings for revenge and for affection, her hatred of the Greece that wronged her and her love of the Greece that is her only home, her possibilities of stony cruelty and her realities of swift self-sacrifice, is a true child of her great and accursed house. The plot is as follows:—Iphigenîa, daughter of Agamemnon, who was supposed to have been sacrificed by her father at Aulis, was really saved by Artemis and is now priestess to that goddess in the land of the Taurians at the extremity of the Friendless Sea. The Taurians are savages who kill all strangers, and if ever a Greek shall land in the wild place it will be her task to prepare him for sacrifice. She lives with this terror hanging over her, and the first Greek that comes is her unknown brother, Orestes. Their recognition of one another is, perhaps, the finest recognition-scene in all Tragedy; and with its sequels of stratagem and escape forms a thrilling play, haunted not, like a tragedy, by the shadow of death but rather by the shadow of homesickness. The characters are Greeks in a far barbarian land, longing for home or even for the Greek sea. The lyrics are particularly fine, and most of them full of sea-light and the clash of waters.

In the same year as the Andromeda came another romantic play, the Helena. It is a good deal like the Iphigenîa in structure, but it is lighter, harder, and more artificial. The romance of Euripides is never quite the easy dreaming of lighter-hearted writers. And the Helena, in which he seems to have attempted a work of mere fancy, is, if we understand it rightly, a rather brilliant failure. Some critics—quite mistakenly in my judgment—have even argued that it is a parody. The plot is based on a variant of the canonical legend about Helen, a variant generally associated with the ancient lyric poet, Stesichorus. Story tells that Stesichorus at one time lost his eyesight and took it into his head that this was a punishment laid on him by the goddess Helen, because he had told the story of her flight with Paris from her husband's house. He wrote a recantation, based on another form of the Helen-legend, in which Helen was borne away by the God Hermes to Egypt and there lived like a true wife till Menelaus came and found her. The being that went with Paris to Troy was only a phantom image of Helen, contrived by the gods in order to bring about the war, and so reduce the wickedness and multitude of mankind. In Euripides' play there is a wicked king of Egypt, who seeks to marry Helen against her will and kills all Greeks who land in his country. The war at Troy is over, and Menelaus, beaten by storms out of his way, is shipwrecked on the coast of Egypt. He and Helen meet, recognize one another, and by the help of the king's sister, who has second sight, contrive to escape. It is hard to say what exactly is wrong with the Helena; and it may only be that we moderns do not know in what spirit to take it. But the illusion is difficult to keep up and the work seems cold. Reality has gone out of it. For one thing, Helen, in her thorough process of rehabilitation, has emerged that most insipid of fancies, a perfectly beautiful and blameless heroine with no character except love of her husband, whom, by the way, she has not seen for seventeen years.

Another large experiment of this time is the Phoenissae, or Tyrian Women (410?). It is the longest Greek tragedy in existence, and covers the greatest stretch of story. Aeschylus, we remember, had the habit of writing true "trilogies"—three continuous dramas, carrying on the same history. The Phoenissae seems like an attempt to run the matter of a whole trilogy into one play. It does not fall into either of the divisions which I have sketched above: it is neither a play of fancy nor yet a realistic tragedy. But even if we had no external tradition of its date we could tell to what part of the author's life it belongs. It is written, as it is conceived, in the large and heroic style; but it shows in the regular manner of this period a general clash of hatreds and frantic ambitions and revenges and cruel statesmanship standing out against the light of a young man's heroism and a mother's and a sister's love. It is like Euripides, too, that this beautiful mother should be Jocasta, whose unknowing incest had made her an abomination in the eyes of orthodox Greece.

The play tells the story of Thebes. The sin of Oedipus and Jocasta is a thing of the past; Oedipus has blinded himself and cursed his children, and they have in course of time imprisoned him in the vaults of the palace. Jocasta still lives. The sons Polyneices and Eteocles have agreed to reign by turns; Polyneices, the elder, has reigned his year and gone abroad to Argos; Eteocles having once got the crown has refused to yield it up. Polyneices comes with an Argive army to lay siege to Thebes and win his rights by war. The drama is developed in a series of great pictures. We have first the Princess Antigone with an old slave looking from the wall out towards the enemy's camp, seeking for a glimpse of her brother. Next comes a man with face hidden and sword drawn stealing through the gates, seeking for Jocasta. It is Polyneices. The mother has induced her sons to have one meeting before they fight. The meeting reveals nothing but ambition and mutual hatred. They agree to look for one another on the field, and Polyneices goes. There are consultations in the beleaguered city. Creon, who is Jocasta's brother and a sort of Prime Minister, advises the rash Eteocles; but the prophets must be consulted too, that the gods may be favourable. The prophet Tiresias—blind and old and jealous, as so often in Greek tragedy—proclaims that the only medicine to save the state is for Creon's son, Menoikeus, to be slain as a sin-offering in the lair of the ancient Dragon whom Cadmus slew. Creon quickly refuses; he dismisses the prophet and arranges for his son to escape from Thebes and fly to the ends of Greece. The boy feigns consent to the plan of escape, but, as soon as his father has left him, rushes enthusiastically up to a tower of the city and flings himself over into the Dragon's den. A messenger comes to Jocasta with news of the battle. "Are her sons slain?" No; both are alive and unhurt. He tells his story of the Argive attack and its repulse from every gate.—"But what of the two brothers?"—He must go now and will bring more news later.—Jocasta sees he is concealing something and compels him to speak. The truth comes out; the brothers are preparing a single combat. With a shriek the mother calls Antigone; and the two women, young and old, make their way through the army to try to separate the blood-mad men. We learn from a second messenger how the brothers have slain each other "in a meadow of wild lotus," and Jocasta has killed herself with one of their swords. Antigone returns and to bring the news to her only friend, the blind Oedipus. Creon by Eteocles' charge takes over the government, he, too, a broken-hearted man, but none the less ruthless; he proclaims that Polyneices' body shall lie unburied and that Oedipus, the source of pollution, shall be cast out of the land; Antigone meantime shall marry Creon's son, Haemon. Antigone defies him. She will not wed Haemon nor any of Creon's kin: her father shall not be cast out to die, for she will go with him and protect him. Polyneices shall not lie unburied, for she herself will return by stealth and bury him. There is still one human love that Oedipus yearns for most; that of the sin-stained wife and mother who is lying dead in the meadow of wild lotus. But meantime he takes the hand of his daughter. Old man and young maiden they go forth together, away from the brutalities of human kind, to the high mountains, to the holy inviolate places on Kithairon where only the wild White Women of Dionysus dance their mystic dances.

The Phoenissae stands half way between the pure Romances and the tragedies of the last period. Of these latter the clearest type is the Electra (probably 413), a play which before it was understood used to receive the unstinted abuse of Critics, as "the meanest of Greek tragedies," "the very worst of all Euripides' plays." It deals with the moral problem of the Blood-Feud, stated in its sharpest terms.

Now the blood-feud, we must realize, in any society where there is no public law and no police, is a high moral duty. A man commits an abominable crime and revels in comfort on the proceeds; his victim is dead, and there is no law which will act automatically. It becomes the duty of some one—normally the heir or representative of the dead man—to devote himself to the work of justice, to forsake all business and pleasure in life till the wrong has been righted and the dead man avenged. A man who would let his kinsman be murdered and then live on at his ease rather than pursue the murderer, would obviously be a poor false creature. Now comes the problem. The strongest possible claim is that of a father murdered; the most horrible act a Greek could conceive was for a man to slay his mother. Suppose a wife murdered her husband, ought her son to slay her? The law of the blood-feud, as traditionally preached from the Temple of Apollo at Delphi, answered, in spite of all repugnances, Yes.

The story had been treated before Euripides by many poets, including Homer, Stesichorus, Pindar, Aeschylus and possibly—though the dates are not certain—Sophocles. Clytemnestra had with the help of her lover Aegisthus murdered her husband Agamemnon; her son Orestes slays her in obedience to Apollo's command, and his sister Electra aids him. Aeschylus in his Libation-Bearers had dealt with this theme on broad lines and with gorgeous intensity of imagination. His Orestes is carried to the deed on a great wave of religious passion and goes mad as soon as it is done. The deed as commanded by God is right, but it is too much for human nature to endure. In an ensuing play Orestes, after long sufferings, is tried for the matricide and, when the human judges are evenly divided, acquitted by the divine voice of Athena. Sophocles treats the subject very differently. He makes a most brilliant play with extraordinary clashes of emotion and moments of tragic beauty. But, evidently of set purpose, he makes the whole treatment hard and archaic. There is no shrinking back, no question of conscience at all. Clytemnestra is a furious tyrant; she beats Electra with her fists, and Aegisthus does worse (1196, 517). The climax of the play is not the mother-murder but the killing of Aegisthus, which was presumably the harder and more exciting job. When Orestes and his friend Pylades come out of the palace streaming with Clytemnestra's blood their nerves are unshaken and the Chorus is careful to say that they are not to be in any way blamed (1423).

The spirit of Euripides is exactly the opposite; so much so indeed that most critics feel clear that the two Electra plays are closely related, and related in opposition. The one is a deliberate protest against the other; unfortunately the play of Sophocles cannot be dated and it is not clear from internal evidence which play was written first.

In the Electra of Euripides we find two main qualities. First, there is psychological realism of the subtlest kind. Secondly, there is a new moral atmosphere. With a power of sympathy and analysis unrivalled in ancient drama he has imagined just what kind of people these children must have been, who would thus through long years nurse the seeds of hatred and at the end kill their mother. He studies them all; Electra, a mixture of heroism and broken nerves; a poisoned and haunted woman, eating her heart in ceaseless broodings of hate and love, both alike unsatisfied; for he suggests, somewhat cruelly, that she might have lived contentedly enough, had she only had a normal married life. The name in its original Doric form suggested the meaning, "Unmated." Orestes is a youth bred in the unwholesome dreams of exile, and now swept away by his sister's stronger will; subject also, as Orestes always is in Greek tragedy, to delusions and melancholy madness. The mother herself is not forgotten, and a most piteous figure she shows, "this sad, middle-aged woman, whose first words are an apology; controlling quickly her old fires, anxious to be as little hated as possible; ready even to atone for her crime, if only there were some safe way of atonement." Thus, in the first place, Euripides has stripped the old bloody deed of the heroic glamour that surrounded it. His actors are not clear-minded heroes moving straight to their purpose. They are human creatures, erring, broken by passion, mastered by their own inhibitions and doubts and regrets. In the second place he has no doubt at all about the ethics of the mother-murder. It was an abomination, and the god who ordained it—if any did—was a power of darkness.

After the deed the two murderers come forth as in Sophocles. But this time they are not triumphant and the Chorus does not hail them as having done right. They reel from the door, "red-garmented and ghastly" and break into a long agony of remorse. The Chorus share their horror. Electra's guilt is the greater since she drove her brother to the deed against his will; even while they love her, they can not quite forget that, though they feel that now at last, by this anguish, her heart may be "made clean within." The play ends with an appearance of the gods. The Heavenly Horsemen, Castor and Polydeuces, who were kinsmen of the dead, appear on a cloud, and speak in judgement and comfort. With a definiteness rare in Euripides they pronounce the deed of vengeance to be evil:

"And Phoebus, Phoebus . . . Nay:
He is my lord, therefore I hold my peace.
But though in light he dwell, not light was this
He showed to thee, but darkness."

Another note is also struck, that of pity for the suffering of humanity. Orestes and Electra, condemned to part, break, as they bid one another farewell, into a great cry, and the gods, hearing it, are shaken:

Alas! what would ye? For that cry
Ourselves and all the sons of heaven
Have pity; yea, our peace is riven
By the strange pain of these that die.

But hark! The far Sicilian sea
Calls, and a noise of men and ships
That labour sunken to the lips
In bitter billows; forth go we
With saving.

They speak such words of comfort and groping wisdom as they can find—no one has ever claimed that they are omniscient—and depart upon their own eternal task, which is not to punish but to save.

The appearance of the gods in the Electra is so beautiful that no critics have yet tried to explain it away as nonsense; and the lesson of it so clear that its meaning is seldom denied. But I find just the same lesson in the final scene of the Orestes, which is commonly taken as the very worst instance of Euripides' habit of closing with a "God from the machine."

The Orestes (408 B.C.) deals with the fate of Orestes some days after his mother's murder. He is mad and sick; his sister is nursing him with devotion. The people have risen against them and they are held prisoners in the palace till an assembly shall try them for murder and pronounce their fate. Meantime Menelaus—Orestes' uncle and king of Sparta—has arrived at the harbour with his wife Helen and their daughter Hermione. He has sent on his wife and daughter to the palace and is expected hourly himself. He is Agamemnon's brother; he has with him an army of Trojan veterans; he can surely be counted on to cow the Argive populace and save his dead brother's son. All our hopes hang on Menelaus, and when at last he comes he proves false. He would like to help; but it would be wrong for him, a foreigner, to dictate to the Argives; and he has only a very small force with him. However, he will reason with Orestes' enemies. One does not forget that, if Argos is left without a king, Menelaus will normally inherit. The sick man blazes into rage against him and Menelaus becomes an open enemy. Exasperation follows on exasperation: Orestes' friend Pylades breaks through the guards and enters the palace to share the prisoners' fate. The assembly hears and at length condemns them. They are given a day in which to die as they best please. Like scorpions surrounded by fire, the three, Orestes, Electra and Pylades, begin to strike blindly. A brilliant idea! They can kill Helen: that will punish Menelaus, and Helen deserves many deaths. Better still, kill Helen and then capture Hermione! Hold a dagger at her throat and then bargain with Menelaus for help even at the last hour! Murder his wife and then force him to help! Splendid! The madness of Orestes infects the whole play. Helen escapes, being half-divine; but they catch Hermione, who, as a matter of fact, has always been kind to them. Menelaus, who has heard news from an escaping slave, rushes up to save Helen, but he finds no sign of her; he finds only the palace barred and the madman on the roof, shrieking derision and holding the knife at his daughter's throat. There is a brief wild attempt at bargaining; then hate in Menelaus overcomes fear. He rejects all terms. Orestes' party sets fire to the palace; and Menelaus at the head of his soldiers beats blindly at the barred gate. "The fire of Hell," to use Dr. Verrall's phrase, has been let loose; rage, hatred, revenge, all blazing to the point of madness; what more can befall?

What does befall is strange and daring. An entry of a god not in gentleness, not with any preparation or introduction, but sudden and terrific, striking all beholders into a trance from which they awaken changed men. The point has not been generally observed, though it is, I think, clear.

At Apollo's first sudden cry "Menelaus, be still!" (line 1625) we know that Orestes is supporting Hermione in one arm while with the other hand he is holding the knife at her throat. He is in exactly the same position at line 1653; he only moves from it at 1671. That is the conduct of a man in a trance, suddenly, as it were, struck rigid. And we shall find that the words spoken by both Menelaus and Orestes when Apollo has finished his charge, are like nothing but the words of men emerging from a trance; a trance, too, of some supernatural kind, like that for instance which falls on the raging world in Mr. Wells's book, In the Days of the Comet. Here, too, a raging world wakes to find itself at peace and its past hatreds unintelligible. And the first thought that comes to the surface is, in each case, the great guiding preoccupation of each man's life; with Menelaus it is Helen; with Orestes the oracle that made him sin. Nay more; when Orestes wakens, half-conscious, to find Hermione lying in his arms, his natural movement, as experiments on hypnotized persons have shown, is to accept the suggestion and draw her to him in love. Greek legend knew well that, as a matter of history, Hermione became Orestes' bride. There is daring, perhaps excessive daring, in making it occur this way; but the psychology of something like hypnotism had a fascination for both Aeschylus and Euripides. For the rest, Apollo has spoken the word of forgiveness and reconciliation. He concludes:

Depart now, each upon his destined way,
Your hates dead and forgotten.

MEN
I obey.

ORESTES
I too; mine heart is as a wine of peace
Poured with the past and thy dark mysteries.

APOLLO

Go now your ways: and without cease
Give honour in your hearts to one,
Of spirits all beneath the sun
Most beautiful; her name is Peace.

I rise with Helen Zeus-ward, past
The orb of many a shining star;
Where Heracles and Hebe are
And Hera, she shall reign at last,

A goddess in men's prayers to be
For ever, with her Brethren twain
Enthronèd, a great help in pain
And queen of the eternal sea.

"Helen a goddess!" say some critics; "the notion is impossible. We have seen her in this same play, a heartless ordinary woman." Yet I think Euripides was serious enough. I do not say he believed either this or any other particular bit of the mythology. But he was writing seriously and aiming at beauty, not at satire. All legend said that Helen was made a goddess; and Euripides was always curiously haunted by the thought of Helen and by the mysterious and deadly power of mere superlative beauty. As Apollo had said to Menelaus (1638):

Thy bride shall be another: none may know

HERMIONE

For the Gods, to work much death and woe,
Devised this loveliness all dreams above,
That men in Greece and Troy for thirst thereof
Should strive and die, and so the old Earth win
Peace from mankind's great multitude and sin.

The superlative beauty may probably enough be found in company with heartlessness and treachery; but cannot these things be purged away, like the hates of Menelaus and Orestes, and the pure beauty remain a thing to pray to and be helped by, much as the old sagas pretend? There is here again the touch of mysticism.

But however it be about Helen, or even about the above explanation in detail of the last scene of the Orestes, it is clear that both the most characteristic plays of the so-called period of gloom end with a strong, almost a mystically strong, note of peace and reconciliation. This note occurs, though with less intensity, at the end of other late plays, such as the Iphigenîa in Tauris and the Helena; and, though without a god, in the Phoenissae. It does not occur at all in the early plays. The Medea and Hecuba end in pure hate; the Hippolytus ends in wonderful beauty and a reconciliation between the hero and his father, who are natural friends, but it keeps up the feud of Aphrodite and Artemis and contains a strange threat of vengeance (v. 1420 ff.) The lovely Thetis of the Andromache brings comfort and rest but preaches no forgiveness; on the contrary the body of Pyrrhus is to be buried at Delphi as an eternal reproach. Euripides all through his life was occupied with the study of revenge. It was a time, as Thucydides tells us, when "men tried to surpass all the record of previous times in the ingenuity of their enterprises and the enormity of their revenges." Euripides seems first to have been almost fascinated by the enormous revenges, at least when they were the work of people who had suffered enormous wrong. He seems, in plays like the Medea, to be saying: "If you goad people beyond endurance, this is the sort of thing you must expect them to do . . . and serve you right!" In the plays after 415 the emphasis has rather changed: "You must expect to be wronged, and revenge will do good to nobody. Seek peace and forgive one another."

CHAPTER VII

MACEDONIA: THE "IPHIGENIA IN AULIS": THE "BACCHAE"

Thus we come round to the figure from which we started, the old sad man with the long beard, who seldom laughed and was not easy to speak to; who sat for long hours in his seaward cave on Salamis, meditating and perhaps writing one could not tell what, except indeed that it was "something great and high." It was natural that he should be sad. His dreams were overthrown; his City, his Beloved, had turned worse than false. Public life was in every way tenfold more intimate and important to an ancient Greek than it is to us moderns who seldom eat a mutton-chop the less when our worst political enemies pass their most detested bills. And Athens had not only been false to her ideals; she had sinned for the sake of success and had then failed. And her failure probably made the daily life of her citizens a thing of anxiety and discomfort. You were never quite sure of your daily food. You were never quite safe from a triumphant raid of the enemy. And the habitual bodily discomfort which is the central fact of old age must have had for Euripides much to aggravate and little to soften it.

It was natural, too, that his people should hate him. Nations at war do not easily forgive those who denounce their wars as unjust; when the war, in spite of all heroism, goes against them, their resentment is all the bitterer. There is, of course, not the ghost of a suggestion in Euripides that he thought the Spartans right or that he wished Athens to be defeated; far from it. But the Athenian public was not in a mood for subtle distinctions, and his air of disapproval was enough. Besides, thought the meaner among them, the man was a known blasphemer. He had been the friend of the sophists; he had denied the gods; worse, he had denounced the doings of the gods as evil. These misfortunes that hurtled round the City's head must surely be sent for some good reason. Very likely just because the City, corrupted by the "charm of words," had allowed such wicked sophists to live? He was at one time prosecuted for impiety; we do not know the date or the details, but he seems to have been acquitted. The day of Socrates had not yet come. But other charges remained. He was a wicked old man: he had preached dreadful things about women; he had defended in his plays adulteresses and perjurers and workers of incest. What must his personal life be, if these were his principles? No wonder that he lived so secretly, he and his wife and that dark-skinned secretary, Cephisophon!

Perhaps he was a miser and had secret stores of wealth? We hear of an action brought against him on these lines. A certain Hygiainon was selected, as a rich man, to perform some "Liturgy" or public service at his own cost, and he claimed that Euripides was richer and should be made to do it instead. We do not know the result of the trial; we only know that the plaintiff attempted to create prejudice against Euripides by quoting the line of the Hippolytus (see above p. 88) which was supposed to defend perjury.

These things were annoyances enough. But there must have been some darker cloud that fell over Euripides' life at this time. For we are not only told in the Lives that "The Athenians bore a grudge against him," and that "he lost patience with the ill-will of his fellow-citizens," but one of our earliest witnesses, Philodemus, says that when he left Athens he did so "in grief, because almost all in Athens were rejoicing over him." The word used means, like the German "Schadenfreude," rejoicing at another's injury. So there must have been some injury for them to rejoice at.

The old Satyrus tradition, with its tone of scandal and misunderstanding, says that his wife was false to him, but the story will not bear historical criticism. And it would not be safe to use so rotten a foundation to build any theory upon, however likely it may be in itself that a man of this kind should meet with domestic unhappiness in one or other of its many forms. In thinking of Euripides one is constantly reminded of Tolstoy. And there are many ways of making husbands miserable besides merely betraying them.

Whatever the cause, shortly after the production of the Orestes in 408 the old poet's endurance snapped, and, at the age apparently of seventy-six, he struck off into voluntary exile. It is only one instance among many of his extraordinary vital force. The language of the ancient Life is unfortunately confused just here, but it seems to say that he went first to Magnesia, with which city he had had relations in earlier days. He had been granted some civic honours there, and had acted as Proxenus—a kind of consul or general protector—for Magnesians in Athens. There was more than one town of the name. But the one meant is probably a large town in the Maeander Valley, not far from Ephesus. It lay in Persian territory, but had been granted by Artaxerxes to the great Themistocles as a gift, and was still ruled, subject to the Persian king, by Themistocles' descendants. Doubtless it was to them that the poet went. We know nothing more, except that he did not stay long in Magnesia, but went on to another place where barbarians or semi-barbarians were ruled by a Greek dynasty.

The king of Macedon, Archelaus, an able despot who was now laying the seeds of the great kingdom which, before the lapse of a century, was to produce Philip and Alexander the Great, had always an eye for men of genius who might be attracted to his court. He had invited Euripides before and now renewed his invitation. Other men of "wisdom" were already with Archelaus. Agathon, the tragic poet; Timotheus, the now famous musician whom Euripides had once saved, so the story ran, from suicide; Zeuxis, the greatest painter of the time; and perhaps also Thucydides, the historian. It would not be like living among barbarians or even uncultivated Greeks. And it is likely enough that the old man hankered for the ease and comfort, for the atmosphere of daily "spoiling," which the royal patron was likely to provide for a lion of such special rarity. For it must have been a little before this time that Greece was ringing with a tale of the value set on Euripides in distant and hostile Sicily. Seven thousand Athenians had been made slaves in Syracuse after the failure of the expedition; and the story now came that some of them had been actually granted their freedom because they were able to recite speeches and choruses of Euripides. Apparently there was no book trade between the warring cities; and the Syracusans could only learn the great poems by word of mouth. Sicily and Macedonia were proud to show that they appreciated the highest poetry better than Athens did.

It was a curious haven that Euripides found. In many ways Macedonia must have been like a great fragment of that Homeric or heroic age from which he had drawn most of his stories. The scenery was all on the grand scale. There were greater plains and forests and rivers, wilder and higher mountain ranges than in the rest of Greece. And the people, though ruled by a dynasty of Greek descent and struggling up towards Hellenism, was still tribal, military and barbaric. A century later we hear of the "old" Macedonian customs. A young man might not dine at the men's tables till he had killed his first wild boar. He had to wear a leathern halter round his waist until he had killed his first man. We hear that when some Macedonian at the court made a rude remark to Euripides the King straightway handed him over to the Athenian to be scourged, a well-meant but embarrassing intervention. And the story told of Euripides' own death, if mythical, is very likely faithful in its local colour. There was a village in Macedonia where some Thracians had once settled and their descendants still lived. One of the king's big Molossian hounds once strayed into this place, and the natives promptly killed and ate her. The king fined the village a talent, which was more than it could possibly pay, and some dreadful fate might have overtaken the dog-eaters had not Euripides interceded and begged them off. And not long afterwards, the story continues, Archelaus was preparing a hunt, and the hungry hounds were set loose. And it so happened that Euripides was sitting alone in a wood outside the city, and the hounds fell on him and tore him to pieces. And behold, these hounds proved to be the children of that Molossian who, through the poet's interference, had died unavenged! The story can hardly be true, or we should hear some echo of it in Aristophanes' Frogs; but no doubt it was the kind of fate that a lonely man might well meet in Macedonia when the king's hounds were astir.

How the poet really died we do not know. We know that he left Athens after the spring of 408, and that he was dead some time before the production of the Frogs in January, 405. And there is reason to believe the story given in the Life that when Sophocles in the previous year was introducing his Chorus in the "Proagon," or Preliminary Appearance, he brought them on without the customary garlands in mourning for his great rival's death. The news, therefore, must have reached Athens by the end of March, 406. Euripides had lived only some eighteen months in Macedon.

The time was not long but it was momentous. After his death three plays were found, Iphigenîa in Aulis, Alcmaeon and Bacchae, sufficiently finished to be put on the stage together by his third son, the Younger Euripides. Two of them are still extant, and one, the Bacchae, remains for all time to testify to the extraordinary return of youth which came to the old poet in his last year. A "lightning before death" if ever there was one!

But let us take first the Iphigenîa in Aulis. It is a play full of problems. We can make out that it was seriously incomplete at the poet's death and was finished by another hand, presumably that of its producer. Unfortunately we do not possess even that version in a complete form. For the archetype of our MSS. was at some time mutilated, and the present end of the play is a patent forgery. But if we allow for these defects, the Iphigenîa in Aulis is a unique and most interesting example of a particular moment in the history of Greek drama. It shows the turning-point between the old fifth century tragedy and the so-called New Comedy which, in the hands of Menander, Philemon and others, dominated the stage of the fourth and third centuries.

Euripides had united two tendencies: on the one hand he had moved towards freedom in metre, realism in character-drawing, variety and adventure in the realm of plot; on the other he had strongly maintained the formal and musical character of the old Dionysiac ritual, making full use of such conventions as the Prologue, the Epiphany, the traditional tragic diction, and above all the Chorus. The New Comedy dropped the chorus, brought the diction close to real life, broke up the stiff forms and revelled in romance, variety, and adventure. Its characters ceased to be legendary Kings and Queens; they became fictional characters from ordinary city life.

The Iphigenîa in Aulis shows an unfinished Euripidean tragedy, much in the manner of the Orestes, completed by a man of some genius whose true ideals were those of modernity and the New Comedy. Two openings of the play are preserved. One is the old stiff Euripidean prologue; the other a fine and vigorous scene of lyric dialogue, which must have suited the taste of the time far better, just as it suits our own. We have early in the play a Messenger; but instead of his entrance being formally prepared and announced in the Euripidean manner, he bursts on to the stage interrupting a speaker in the middle of a verse and the middle of a sentence. There are also peculiarities of metre, such as the elision of -ai, which are unheard of in tragic dialogue but regular in the more conversational style of the New Comedy.

The plot runs thus.—It is night in the Greek camp at Aulis; Agamemnon calls an Old Slave outside his tent and gives him secretly a letter to carry to Clytemnestra. She is at home, and has been directed in previous letters to send her daughter, Iphigenîa, to Aulis to be wedded to Achilles. This letter simply bids her not send the girl.—The Old Slave is bewildered; "What does it mean?" It means that the marriage with Achilles was a blind. Achilles knew nothing of it. It was a plot to get Iphigenîa to the camp and there slaughter her as a sacrifice for the safe passage of the fleet. So Calchas, the priest, had commanded and he was backed by Odysseus and Menelaus. Agamemnon had been forced into compliance, and is now resolved to go back upon his word. The Old Slave goes. Presently comes the entrance of the Chorus, women of Aulis who are dazzled and thrilled by the spectacle of the great army and the men who are prepared to die overseas for the honour of Hellas. But we hear a scuffle outside, and the Old Slave returns pursued by Menelaus, who seizes the letter. He calls for help. Agamemnon comes out and commands Menelaus to give the letter back. A violent scene ensues between the brothers, each telling the other home truths. Menelaus's besotted love for his false wife, his reckless selfishness and cruelty; Agamemnon's consuming ambition, his falseness and weakness, his wish to run with the hare and hunt with the hounds, are all laid bare in a masterly quarrel scene. At last Agamemnon flatly refuses to give his daughter: "Let the army break up, let Menelaus go without his accursed wife, and the barbarians laugh as loudly as they will! Agamemnon will not have his child slain and his own heart broken to please any one." "Is that so?" says Menelaus: "Then I go straight to. . . ." He is interrupted by a Messenger who announces that Iphigenîa has come and her mother, Clytemnestra, is with her. Agamemnon sends them a formal message of welcome; dismisses the Messenger, and then bursts into tears. This shakes Menelaus; he hesitates; then abruptly says, "I cannot force you. Save the girl as best you can." But now it is too late. The army knows that the Queen has come; Calchas and Odysseus know. Agamemnon has lost the power of action. The next scene is between the mother, father and daughter; Clytemnestra, full of questions about the marriage, Iphigenîa full of excitement and shy tenderness, which expresses itself in special affectionateness towards her father. He tries to persuade Clytemnestra to go home and leave the child with him; she is perplexed and flatly refuses to go.

The next scene is close to comedy, though comedy of a poignant kind. Achilles, knowing naught of all these plots and counter-plots, comes to tell the General that his men—the Myrmidons—are impatient and want to sail for Troy at once. At the door of the tent he meets Clytemnestra, who greets him with effusive pleasure and speaks of "the marriage that is about to unite them." The young soldier is shy, horrified, anxious to run away from this strange lady who is so more than friendly, when suddenly a whisper through the half-closed door startles them. "Is the coast clear? Yes?"—then the whisperer will come. It is the Old Slave, who can bear it no more but reveals the whole horrible plot; Iphigenîa is to be slaughtered by the priests; the marriage with Achilles was a bait for deceiving Clytemnestra. —Clytemnestra is thunderstruck, Achilles furious with rage. "He is dishonoured; he is made a fool of. What sort of man do they take him for, to use his name thus without his authority? Why could not they ask his consent? They could sacrifice a dozen girls for all he cares, and he would not have stood in the way. But now they have dishonoured him, and he will forbid the sacrifice. . . ." Clytemnestra, who has watched like a drowning woman to see which way the youth's fierce vanity would leap, throws herself at his feet in gratitude; "Shall her daughter, also, come and embrace his knees?" No; Achilles does not want any woman to kneel to him. Let the women try to change Agamemnon's mind; if they can do it, all is well. If not, Achilles will fight to the last to save the girl.

There follows the inevitable scene in which mother and daughter—the latter inarticulate with tears—convict the father and appeal to him. A fine scene it is, in which each character comes out clear, and through the still young and obedient Clytemnestra one descries the shadow of the great murderess to be. Agamemnon is broken but helpless. It is too late to go back.

The two women are left weeping at the door of the tent, when they hear a sound of tumult. It is Achilles, and men behind stoning him. Iphigenîa's first thought is to fly; she dare not look Achilles in the face. Yet she stays. Achilles enters. The whole truth has come out; the army clamours for the sacrifice and is furious against him. . . . "Will not his own splendid Myrmidons protect him?"—"It is they who were the first to stone him! Nevertheless he will fight. He has his arms. Clytemnestra must fight too; cling to her daughter by main force when they come, as they presently will, to drag her to the altar. . . ." "Stay!" says Iphigenîa: "Achilles must not die for her sake. What is her miserable life compared with his? One man who can fight for Hellas is worth ten thousand women, who can do nothing. Besides, she has been thinking it over; she has seen the great gathered army, ready to fight and die for a cause, and, like the Chorus, has fallen under the spell of it. She realizes that it lies with her, a weak girl, to help them to victory. All great Hellas is looking to her; and she is proud and glad to give her life for Hellas."—It is a beautiful and simple speech. And the pride of Achilles withers up before it. In a new tone he answers: "God would indeed have made him blessed if he had won her for his wife. As it is, Iphigenîa is right. . . ." Yet he offers still to fight for her and save her. She does not know what death is; and he loves her.—She answers that her mind is made up. "Do not die for me, but leave me to save Hellas, if I can." Achilles yields. Still he will go and stand beside the altar, armed; if at the last moment she calls to him, he is ready. So he goes. The mother and daughter bid one another a last farewell, and with a song of triumph Iphigenîa, escorted by her maidens, goes forth to meet the slaughterers. . . . Here the authentic part of our play begins to give out. There are fragments of a messenger's speech afterwards, and it is likely on the whole that Artemis saved the victim, as is assumed in the other Iphigenîa play.

The Iphigenîa in Aulis, in spite of its good plot, is not really one of Euripides' finest works; yet, if nothing else of his were preserved, it would be enough to mark him out as a tremendous power in the development of Greek literature. Readers who enjoy drama but have never quite accustomed themselves to the stately conventions of fifth century tragedy very often like it better than any other Greek play. It is curiously different from its twin sister the Bacchae.

A reader of the Bacchae who looks back at the ritual sequence described above (p. 64) will be startled to find how close this drama, apparently so wild and imaginative, has kept to the ancient rite. The regular year-sequence is just clothed in sufficient myth to make it a story. The daemon must have his enemy who is like himself; then we must have the Contest, the Tearing Asunder, the Messenger, the Lamentation mixed with Joy-cries, the Discovery of the scattered members—and by a sort of doubling the Discovery of the true God—and the Epiphany of the Daemon in glory. All are there in the Bacchae. The god Dionysus, accompanied by his Wild Women, comes to his own land and is rejected by his kinsman, King Pentheus, and by the women of the royal house. The god sends his divine madness on the women. The wise Elders of the tribe warn the king; but Pentheus first binds and imprisons the god; then yielding gradually to the divine power, agrees to go disguised in woman's garb to watch the secret worship of the Maenads on Mt. Kithairon. He goes, is discovered by the Maenads and torn in fragments. His mother, Agave, returns in triumph dancing with her son's head, which, in her madness, she takes for a lion's. There is Lamentation mixed with mad Rejoicing. The scattered body is recovered; Agave is restored to her right mind and to misery; the god appears in majesty and pronounces doom on all who have rejected him. The mortals go forth to their dooms, still faithful, still loving one another. The ghastly and triumphant god ascends into heaven. The whole scheme of the play is given by the ancient ritual. It is the original subject of Attic tragedy treated once more, as doubtless it had already been treated by all or almost all the other tragedians.

But we can go further. We have enough fragments and quotations from the Aeschylean plays on this subject—especially the Lycurgus trilogy—to see that all kinds of small details which seemed like invention, and rather fantastic invention, on the part of Euripides, are taken straight from Aeschylus or the ritual or both. The timbrels, the fawnskin, the ivy, the sacred pine, the god taking the forms of Bull and Lion and Snake; the dances on the mountain at dawn; the Old Men who are by the power of the god made young again; the god represented as beardless and like a woman; the god imprisoned and escaping; the earthquake that wrecks Pentheus' palace; the victim Pentheus disguised as a woman; all these and more can be shown to be in the ritual and nearly all are in the extant fragments of Aeschylus. Even variants of the story which have been used by previous poets have somehow a place found for them. There was, for instance, a variant which made Pentheus lead an army against the Wild Women; in the Bacchae this plan is not used, but Pentheus is made to think of it and say he will perhaps follow it, and Dionysus is made to say what will happen if he does. (Aesch. Eum. 25 f.; Bac. 50 ff. 809, 845.) There never was a great play so steeped in tradition as the Bacchae.

The Iphigenîa was all invention, construction, brilliant psychology; it was a play of new plot and new characters. The Bacchae takes an old fixed plot, and fixed formal characters: Dionysus, Pentheus, Cadmus, Teiresias, they are characters that hardly need proper names. One might just as well call them—The God, the Young King, the Old King, the Prophet; and as for Agave, our MSS. do as a rule simply call her "Woman." The Iphigenîa is full of informalities, broken metres, interruptions. Its Chorus hardly matters to the plot and has little to sing. The Bacchae is the most formal Greek play known to us; its Chorus is its very soul and its lyric songs are as long as they are magnificent. For the curious thing is that in this extreme of formality and faithfulness to archaic tradition Euripides has found both his greatest originality and his most perfect freedom.

He is re-telling an old story; but he is not merely doing that. In the Bacchae almost every reader feels that there is something more than a story. There is a meaning, or there is at least a riddle. And we must try in some degree to understand it. Now, in order to keep our heads cool, it is first necessary to remember clearly two things. The Bacchae is not free invention; it is tradition. And it is not free personal expression, it is drama. The poet cannot simply and without a veil state his own views; he can only let his own personality shine through the dim curtain in front of which his puppets act their traditional parts and utter their appropriate sentiments. Thus it is doubly elusive. And therein no doubt lay its charm to the poet. He had a vehicle into which he could pour many of those "vaguer faiths and aspirations which a man feels haunting him and calling to him, but which he cannot state in plain language or uphold with a full acceptance of responsibility." But our difficulties are even greater than this. The personal meaning of a drama of this sort is not only elusive; it is almost certain to be inconsistent with itself or at least incomplete. For one only feels its presence strongly when in some way it clashes with the smooth flow of the story.

Let us imagine a great free-minded modern poet—say Swinburne or Morris or Victor Hugo, all of whom did such things—making for some local anniversary a rhymed play in the style of the old Mysteries on some legend of a mediaeval saint. The saint, let us suppose, is very meek and is cruelly persecuted by a wicked emperor, whom he threatens with hell fire; and at the end let us have the emperor in the midst of that fire and the saint in glory saying, "What did I tell you?" And let us suppose that the play in its course gives splendid opportunities for solemn Latin hymns, such as Swinburne and Hugo delighted in. We should probably have a result something like the Bacchae.

For one thing, in such a play one would not be troubled by little flaws and anachronisms and inconsistencies. One would not be shocked to hear St. Thomas speaking about Charlemagne, or to find the Mouth of Hell situated in the same street as the emperor's lodging. Just so we need not be shocked in the Bacchae to find that, though the god is supposed to be appearing for the first time in Thebes, his followers appeal to "immemorial custom" as the chief ground for their worship (201, 331, 370: cf. Aesch. fr. 22?), nor to observe that the Chorus habitually makes loud professions of faith under the very nose of the tyrant without his ever attending to them (263 f., 328 f., 775 f.). Nor even that the traditional earthquake which destroys the palace causes a good deal of trouble in the thinking out. It had to be there; it was an integral part of the story in Aeschylus (fr. 58), and in all probability before him. One may suppose that the Greek stage carpenter was capable of some symbolic crash which served its purpose. The language used is carefully indefinite. It suggests that the whole palace is destroyed, but leaves a spectator free, if he so chooses, to suppose that it is only the actual prison of Dionysus, which is "off-stage" and unseen. In any case the ruins are not allowed to litter the stage and, once over, the earthquake is never noticed or mentioned again.

Again, such a play would involve a bewildering shift of sympathy, just as the Bacchae does. At first we should be all for the saint and against the tyrant; the persecuted monks with their hymns of faith and endurance would stir our souls. Then, when the tables were turned and the oppressors were seen writhing in Hell, we should feel that, at their worst, they did not quite deserve that: we should even begin to surmise that perhaps, with all their faults, they were not really as horrible as the saint himself, and reflect inwardly what a barbarous thing, after all, this mediaeval religion was.

This bewildering shift of sympathy is common in Euripides. We have had it before in such plays as the Medea and Hecuba: oppression generates revenge, and the revenge becomes more horrible than the original oppression. In these plays the poet offers no solution. He gives us only the bitterness of life and the unspoken "tears that are in things." The first serious attempt at a solution comes in the Electra and Orestes.

In a Mystery-play such as we have imagined, re-told by a great modern poet, the interest and meaning would hardly lie in the main plot. They would lie in something which the poet himself contributed. We might, for instance, find that he had poured all his soul into the Latin hymns, or into the spectacle of the saint, alone and unterrified, defying all the threats and all the temptations which the Emperor can bring to bear upon him. There might thus be a glorification of that mystic rejection of the world which lies at the heart of mediaeval monasticism, without the poet for a moment committing himself to a belief in monasticism or an acceptance of the Catholic Church.

We have in the Bacchae—it seems to me impossible to deny it—a heartfelt glorification of "Dionysus." No doubt it is Dionysus in some private sense of the poet's own; something opposed to "the world"; some spirit of the wild woods and the sunrise, of inspiration and untrammelled life. The presentation is not consistent, however magical the poetry. At one moment we have the Bacchantes raving for revenge, at the next they are uttering the dreams of some gentle and musing philosopher. A deliberate contrast seems to be made in each Chorus between the strophe and the antistrophe. It is not consistent; though it is likely enough that, if one had taxed Euripides with the contradiction, he might have had some answer that would surprise us. His first defence, of course, would be a simple one; it is not the playwright's business to have any views at all; he is only re-telling a traditional story and trying to tell it right. But he might also venture outside his defences and answer more frankly: "This spirit that I call Dionysus, this magic of inspiration and joy, is it not as a matter of fact the great wrecker of men's lives?

While life seems a decent grey to you all over, you are safe and likely to be prosperous; when you feel the heavens opening, you may begin to tremble. For the vision you see there, as it is the most beautiful of things, is likely also to be the most destructive." For the poet himself, indeed, the only course is to pursue it across the world to the cold mountain tops (410 ff.):

For there is Grace, and there is the Heart's Desire,
And peace to adore Thee,
Thou spirit of guiding fire!

He will clasp it even though it slay him.

The old critics used to assume that the Bacchae marked a sort of repentance. The veteran free-lance of thought, the man who had consistently denounced and ridiculed all the foul old stories of mythology, now saw the error of his ways and was returning to orthodoxy. Such a view strikes us now as almost childish in its incompetence. Yet there is, I think, a gleam of muddled truth somewhere behind it. There was no repentance; there was no return to orthodoxy; nor indeed was there, in the strict sense, any such thing as "orthodoxy" to return to. For Greek religion had no creeds. But there is, I think, a rather different attitude towards the pieties of the common man.

It is well to remember that, for all his lucidity of language, Euripides is not lucid about religion. His general spirit is clear: it is a spirit of liberation, of moral revolt, of much denial; but it is also a spirit of search and wonder and surmise. He was not in any sense a "mere" rationalist. We find in his plays the rule of divine justice often asserted, sometimes passionately denied; and one tragedy, the Bellerophontes, is based on the denial. It is in a fragment of this play that we have the outcry of some sufferer:

Doth any feign there is a God in heaven?
There is none, none!

And afterwards the hero, staggered by the injustice of things, questions Zeus himself and is, for answer, blasted by the thunderbolt. A clearer form of this same question, and one which vexed the age a good deal, was to ask whether or no the world is governed by some great Intelligence or Understanding ("Sunesis"), or, more crudely, whether the gods are "sunetoi." Euripides at times "hath deep in his hope a belief in some Understanding," and is represented in the Frogs as actually praying to it by that name; but he sometimes finds the facts against him (Hippolytus, 1105; Frogs, 893; Iph. Aul., 394a; Her., 655; Tro., 884 ff., compared with the sequel of the play). The question between polytheism and monotheism, which has loomed so large to some minds, never troubled him. He uses the singular and plural quite indifferently, and probably his "gods," when used as identical with "God" or "the Divine," would hardly even suggest to him the gods of mythology. If one is to venture a conjecture, his own feeling may, perhaps, be expressed by a line in the Orestes (418):

We are slaves of gods, whatever gods may be.

That is, there are unknown forces which shape or destroy man's life, and which may be conceived as in some sense personal. But morally, it would seem, these forces are not better, but less good, than man, who at least loves and pities and tries to understand. Such is the impression, I think, left on readers of the Bacchae, the Hippolytus or the Trojan Women.

But there is one thought which often recurs in Euripides in plays of all periods, and is specially thrown in his teeth by Aristophanes. That satirist, when piling up Euripides' theatrical iniquities, takes as his comic climax "women who say Life is not Life." The reference is to passages like fr. 833, from the Phrixus:

Who knoweth if the thing that we call death
Be Life, and our Life dying—who knoweth?
Save only that all we beneath the sun
Are sick and suffering, and those foregone
Not sick, nor touched with evil any more.

(Cf. fr. 638, 816; also Helena, 1013; Frogs, 1082, 1477). The idea recurs again and again, as also does the thought that death is "some other shape of life" in the Medea and even in the Ion (Med., 1039; Ion, 1068). Nay, more, death may be the state that we unconsciously long for, and that really fulfils our inmost desires: "There is no rest on this earth," says a speaker in the Hippolytus (191 f.),

"And whatever far-off state there be,
Dearer than Life to mortality,
The hand of the Dark hath hold thereof
And mist is under and mist above:

and thus," she continues, "we cling to this strange thing that shines in the sunlight, and are sick with love for it, because we have not seen beyond the veil." A stirring thought this, and much nearer to the heart of mysticism than any mere assertion of human immortality. Thus it is not from any position like what we should call "dogmatic atheism" or "scientific materialism" that the child of the Sophists started his attacks on the current mythology. The Sophists themselves had no orthodoxy.

Euripides was always a rejecter of the Laws of the Herd. He was in protest against its moral standards, its superstitions and follies, its social injustices; in protest also against its worldliness and its indifference to those things which, both as a poet and a philosopher, he felt to be highest. And such he remained throughout his life. But in his later years the direction of his protest did, I think, somewhat change. In the Athens of Melos and the Sicilian expedition there was something that roused his aversion far more than did the mere ignorance of a stupid Greek farmer. It was a deeper "amathia," a more unteachable brutality. The men who spoke in the Melian Dialogue were full of what they considered "Sophia." It is likely enough that they conformed carefully to the popular religious prejudices—such politicians always do: but in practice they thought as little of "the gods" as the most pronounced sceptic could wish. They had quite rejected such unprofitable ideals as "pity and charm of words and the generosity of strength," to which the simple man of the old times had always had the door of his heart open. They were haunters of the market-place, mockers at all simplicity, close pursuers of gain and revenge; rejecters, the poet might feel in his bitterness, both of beauty and of God. And the Herd, as represented by Athens, followed them. Like other ideal democrats he turned away from the actual Demos, which surrounded him and howled him down, to a Demos of his imagination, pure and uncorrupted, in which the heart of the natural man should speak. His later plays break out more than once into praises of the unspoiled countryman, neither rich nor poor, who works with his own arm and whose home is "the solemn mountain" not the city streets (cf. especially Orestes, 917-922, as contrasted with 903 ff.; also the Peasant in the Electra; also Bac., 717). In the Bacchae we have not only several denunciations—not at all relevant to the main plot—of those whom the world calls "wise"; we have the wonderful chorus about the fawn escaped from the hunters, rejoicing in the green and lonely places where no pursuing voice is heard and the "little things of the woodland" live unseen. (866 ff.) That is the poetry of this emotion. The prose of it comes in a sudden cry:

The simple nameless herd of humanity
Have deeds and faith that are truth enough for me;

though even that prose has followed immediately on the more mystical doctrine that man must love the Day and the Night, and that Dionysus has poured the mystic Wine that is Himself for all things that live (421-431, 284). In another passage, which I translate literally, he seems to make his exact position more clear: "As for Knowledge, I bear her no grudge; I take joy in the pursuit of her. But the other things" (i.e., the other elements of existence) "are great and shining. Oh, for Life to flow towards that which is beautiful, till man through both light and darkness should be at peace and reverent, and, casting from him Laws that are outside Justice, give glory to the gods!"

Those "Laws which are outside Justice" would make trouble enough between Euripides and the "simple herd" if ever they reached the point of discussing them. He who most loves the ideal Natural Man seldom agrees with the majority of his neighbours. But for the meantime the poet is wrapped up in another war, in which he and religion and nature and the life of the simple man seem to be standing on one side against a universal enemy.

I am not attempting to expound the whole meaning of the Bacchae. I am only suggesting a clue by which to follow it. Like a live thing it seems to move and show new faces every time that, with imagination fully working, one reads the play. There were many factors at work, doubtless, to produce the Bacchae: the peculiar state of Athens, the poet's ecstasy of escape from an intolerable atmosphere, the simple Homeric life in Macedonian forests and mountains, and perhaps even the sight of real Bacchantes dancing there. But it may be that the chief factor is simply this. When a man is fairly confronted with death and is consciously doing his last work in the world, the chances are that, if his brain is clear and unterrified, the deepest part of his nature will assert itself. Euripides was both a reasoner and a poet. The two sides of his nature sometimes clashed and sometimes blended. But ever since the Heracles he had known which service he really lived for; and in his last work it is the poet who speaks, and reveals, so far as such a thing can be revealed, the secret religion of poetry.

CHAPTER VIII

THE ART OF EURIPIDES: IDEAL FORM AND SINCERE SPIRIT: PROLOGUE: MESSENGER: "DEUS EX MÂCHINÂ"

Euripides was so much besides a poet that we sometimes tend to regard him exclusively as a great thinker or a great personality and forget that it is in his poetry that he lives. A biography like that which we have attempted to sketch is of little value except as a kind of clue to guide a reader through the paths of the poet's own work. It is only by reading his plays that we can know him; and unfortunately, owing to the two thousand odd years that have passed since his death, we must needs approach them through some distorting medium. We read them either in a foreign language, as a rule most imperfectly understood, or else in a translation. It is hard to say by which method a reader who is not a quite good Greek scholar will miss most. A further difficulty occurs about the translations. I need not perhaps apologize for assuming normally in the present volume the use of my own. There has been lately, since the work of Verrall in England and Wilamowitz in Germany, a far more successful effort made to understand the mind of Euripides, while the recent performances of his plays in London and elsewhere have considerably increased our insight into his stagecraft. Consequently we can now see that the older translations, even when verbally defensible and even skilful, are often seriously inadequate or misleading. A comparison of Dr. Verrall's English version of the Ion with practically any of its predecessors will illustrate this point.

The greatest change that has come over our study of Greek civilization and literature in the last two generations is this: that we now try to approach it historically, as a thing that moves and grows and has its place in the whole life-history of man. The old view, sometimes called classicist, was to regard the great classical books as eternal models; their style was simply the right style, and all the variations observable in modern literature were, in one degree or another, so many concessions to the weakness of human nature. There is in this view an element of truth. The fundamental ideals which have produced results so singularly and so permanently successful cannot be lightly disregarded. Books that are still read with delight after two thousand years are certainly, in some sense, models to imitate. But the great flaw in the classicist view, as regards the ancient literature itself, was that it concentrated attention on the external and accidental; on the mannerism, not the meaning; on the temporary fashion of a great age, not on the spirit which made that age great. A historical mind will always try, by active and critical use of the imagination, to see the Greek poet or philosopher in his real surroundings and against his proper background. Seen thus he will appear, not as a stationary "ancient" contrasted with a "modern," but as a moving and striving figure, a daring pioneer in the advance of the human spirit, fore-doomed to failure because his aims were so far greater than his material resources, his habit of mind so far in advance of the world that surrounded him. We seem in ancient Greece to be moving in a region that is next door to savagery, and in the midst of it to have speech with men whom we might gladly accept as our leaders or advisers if they lived now.

Meantime there are screens between us and these men; the screens of a foreign language, a strange form of life, different conventions in art. It is these last that we must now deal with, for we shall find it hard ever to understand Greek tragedy if we expect from it exactly what we expect from a modern or Elizabethan play.

One would have to make no such preface if we were dealing with the form of Greek Drama that immediately succeeded the great age of Tragedy. There arose in the fourth century, B.C., a kind of play that we could understand at once, the so-called New Comedy of Menander and Philemon. New Comedy is neither tragic nor comic, but, like our own plays, a discreet mixture of both. It has no austere religious atmosphere. Its interest—like ours—is in love and adventure and intrigue. It has turned aside from legend and legendary Kings and Queens, and operates, as we do, with a boldly invented plot and fictitious characters, drawn mostly from everyday life. The New Comedy dominated the later Attic stage and called into life the Roman. It was highly praised and immensely popular. It was so easy in its flow and it demanded so little effort. Yet, significantly enough, it has passed away without leaving a single complete specimen of its work in existence. When after ages were exerting themselves to save from antiquity just that minimum of most precious things that must not be allowed to die, it was the greater and more difficult form of drama that they preserved.

Let us try to see and to surmount the difficulties. Every form of art has its conventions. Think, for instance, of the conventions of modern Opera. Looked at in cold blood, from outside the illusion, few forms of art could be more absurd, yet, I suppose, the emotional and artistic effect of a great opera is extraordinarily high. The analogy may help us in the understanding of Greek tragedy.

Let us remember that it is at heart a religious ritual. We shall then understand—so far as it is necessary for a modern reader to think of such things—the ceremonial dress, the religious masks, the constant presence or nearness of the supernatural. We shall understand, perhaps, also the formal dignity of language and action. It is verse and, like all Greek verse, unrhymed; but it is not at all like the loose go-as-you-please Elizabethan verse, which fluctuates from scene to scene and makes up for its lack of strict form by extreme verbal ornamentation. In Greek tragic dialogue the metrical form is stiff and clear; hardly ever could a tragic line by any mistake be taken for prose; the only normal variation is not towards prose but towards a still more highly wrought musical lyric. Yet inside the stiff metrical form the language is clear, simple and direct. A similar effect can, in my opinion, only be attained in English by the use of rhyme. You must somehow feel always that you are in the realm of verse, yet your language must always be simple. In blank verse the language has to be tortured a little, or it will read like prose.

Now all this sounds highly conventional; that it is. And artificial and unreal? That it is not. We are apt at the present moment of taste to associate together two things that have no real connexion with one another—sincerity of thought and sloppiness of form. Take on the one hand dramatic poems like Swinburne's Locrine, written all in rhymed verse and partly in sonnets, or George Meredith's Modern Love, which is all in a form of sonnet. These are works of the most highly-wrought artistic convention; their form is both severe and elaborate; in that lies half their beauty. But the other half lies in their sincerity and delicacy of thought and their intensity of feeling. They are sincere but not formless. Of the other extreme, which is formless without being sincere, I need give no examples. The reader can think of the worst-written novel he knows and it will probably satisfy the conditions. In Greek tragedy we have the element of formal convention extremely strong; we have also great subtlety and sincerity.

This quality of sincerity is, perhaps, the very first thing that should be pointed out to a reader who is beginning Greek tragedy. Coming in the midst of so much poetical convention it takes a modern reader by surprise; he expected romantic idealism and he finds clear character-drawing. I once read a critic who argued that Euripides had low ideals of womanhood because, in the critic's carefully pondered judgment, Medea was not a perfect wife. Even Coleridge complained that the Greek tragedians could not make a heroine interesting without "un-sexing her." Such criticisms imply a conception of drama in which the women are conventionally seen through a roseate mist of amatory emotion. We mean to be in love with the heroine, and in order that she may be worthy of that honour the author must endow her with all the adorable attributes. The men in such plays suffer much less from beautification, but even they suffer. This spurious kind of romanticism implies chiefly an indifference to truth in the realm of character; it is generally accompanied by an indifference to truth in other respects. It leads stage-writers to look out for the effect, not the truth; to write with a view to exciting the audience instead of expressing something which they have to express. It leads in fact to all the forms of staginess. Now from Greek tragedy this kind of falseness is almost entirely absent. "It has no utter villains, no insipidly angelic heroines. Even its tyrants generally have some touch of human nature about them; they have at least a case to state. Even its virgin martyrs are not waxen images." The stories are no doubt often miraculous; the characters themselves are often in their origin supernatural. But their psychology is severely true. It is not the psychology of melodrama, specially contrived to lead up to "situations." It is that of observed human nature, and human nature not merely observed but approached with a serious almost reverent sympathy and an unlimited desire to understand. Mr. Bernard Shaw, in his Quintessence of Ibsenism (1913), writes of a new element brought into modern drama by the Norwegian school. "Ibsen was grim enough in all conscience; no man has said more terrible things; and yet there is not one of Ibsen's characters who is not, in the old phrase, the temple of the Holy Ghost, and who does not move you at moments by the sense of that mystery." Allowing for the great difference of treatment and the comparative absence of detail in the ancient drama, this phrase would, I think, be true of all the great Greek tragedians. In Euripides it is clear enough. Jason, as well as Medea, Clytemnestra as well as Electra, even satirized characters like Menelaus in the Trojan Women or Agamemnon in the Iphigenîa in Aulis, are creatures of one blood with ourselves; they are beings who must be understood, who cannot be thrust beyond the pale; and they all "move us at moments by the sense of that mystery." But it holds in general for the other tragedians too, for the creators of Creon and Antigone, of Prometheus and Zeus. "What poet until quite modern times would have dared to make an audience sympathize with Clytemnestra, the blood-stained adulteress, as Aeschylus does? Who would have dared, like Sophocles, to make Antigone speak cruelly to her devoted sister, or Electra, with all our sympathies concentrated upon her, behave like a wild beast and be disgusted with herself for so doing? (Soph. Elec. 616 ff.)."

But what we have now to realize is that this sincerity of treatment takes place inside a shell of stiff and elaborate convention.

At the very beginning of a play by Euripides we shall find something that seems deliberately calculated to offend us and destroy our interest: a Prologue. It is a long speech with no action to speak of; and it tells us not only the present situation of the characters—which is rather dull—but also what is going to happen to them—which seems to us to spoil the rest of the play. And the modern scholastic critic says in his heart, "Euripides had no sense of the stage."

Now, since we know that he had a very great sense of the stage and enormous experience also, let us try to see what value he found in this strange prologue. First, no doubt it was a convenience. There were no playbills to hand round, with lists of the dramatis personae. Also, a Greek tragedy is always highly concentrated; it consists generally of what would be the fifth act of a modern tragedy, and does not spend its time on explanatory and introductory acts. The Prologue saved time here. But why does it let out the secret of what is coming? Why does it spoil the excitement beforehand? Because, we must answer, there is no secret, and the poet does not aim at that sort of excitement. A certain amount of plot-interest there certainly is: we are never told exactly what thing will happen but only what sort of thing; or we are told what will happen but not how it will happen. But the enjoyment which the poet aims at is not the enjoyment of reading a detective story for the first time; it is that of reading Hamlet or Paradise Lost for the second or fifth or tenth. When Hippolytus or Oedipus first appears on the stage you know that he is doomed; that knowledge gives an increased significance to everything that he says or does; you see the shadow of disaster closing in behind him, and when the catastrophe comes it comes with the greater force because you were watching for it.

"At any rate," the modern reader may persist: "the prologue is rather dull. It does not arrest the attention, like, for instance, the opening scenes of Macbeth or Julius Caesar or Romeo and Juliet." No; it does not. Shakespeare, one may suppose, had a somewhat noisy audience, all talking among themselves and not disposed to listen till their attention was captured by force. The Greek audience was, as far as we can make out, sitting in a religious silence. A prayer had been offered and incense burnt on the altar of Dionysus, and during such a ritual the rule enjoined silence. It was not necessary for the Greek poet to capture his audience by a scene of bustle or excitement. And this left him free to do two things, both eminently characteristic of Greek art. He could make his atmosphere and he could build up his drama from the ground.

Let us take the question of building first. If you study a number of modern plays, you will probably find that their main "effects" are produced in very different places, though especially of course at the fall of each curtain. A good Greek play moves almost always in a curve of steadily increasing tension—increasing up to the last scene but one and then, as a rule, sinking into a note of solemn calm. It often admits a quiet scene about the middle to let the play take breath; but it is very chary indeed of lifting and then dropping again, and never does so without definite reason. In pursuance of this plan, Euripides likes to have his opening as low-toned, as still, as slow in movement, as he can make it: its only tension is a feeling of foreboding or of mystery. It is meant as a foundation to build upon, and every scene that follows will be higher, swifter, more intense. A rush of excitement at the opening would jar, so to speak, the whole musical scheme.

And this quiet opening is especially used to produce the right state of mind in the audience—or, as our modern phrase puts it, to give the play its atmosphere. Take almost any opening: the Suppliant Women, with its band of desolate mothers kneeling at an altar and holding the Queen prisoner while she speaks: the Andromache, the Heracles, the Children of Heracles almost the same—an altar and helpless people kneeling at it—kneeling and waiting: the Trojan Women with its dim-seen angry gods; the Hecuba with its ruined city walls and desolate plain and the ghost of the murdered Polydorus brooding over them; the Hippolytus with its sinister goddess, potent and inexorable, who vanishes at the note of the hunting horn but is felt in the background throughout the whole play; the Iphigenîa, with its solitary and exiled priestess waiting at the doors of her strange temple of death. Most of the prologues have about them something supernatural; all of them something mysterious; and all of them are scenes of waiting, not acting—waiting till the atmosphere can slowly gain its full hold. Regarded from this point of view I think that every opening scene in Greek tragedy will be seen to have its significance and its value in the whole scheme of the play. Certainly the prologue generally justifies itself in the acting.

And when the prologue is over and the action begins, we need not expect even then any rapid stir or bustle. Dr. Johnson has told us that a man who should read Richardson for the story might as well hang himself; the same fate might overtake one who sate at Greek tragedies expecting them to hurry at his bidding. The swift rush will come, sure enough, swift and wild with almost intolerable passion; but it will not come anywhere near the first scenes. We shall have a dialogue in longish speeches, each more or less balanced against its fellow, beautiful no doubt and perhaps moving, but slow as music is slow. Or we shall have a lyrical scene, strophe exactly balanced against antistrophe, more beautiful but slower still in its movement, and often at first hearing a little difficult to follow. Poetry is there and drama is there, and character and plot interest; but often they are unrolled before you not as things immediately happening, but as things to feel and reflect upon. It is a bigger world than ours and every movement in it is slower and larger.

And when the poet wants to show us the heroine's state of mind his method will be quite different from ours. We should rack our brains to compose a "natural" dialogue in which her state of mind would appear, or we should make her best friend explain what she is like, or we should invent small incidents to throw light upon her. And our language would all the time be carefully naturalistic; not a bit—or, if the poet within us rebels, hardly a bit—more dignified than the average diction of afternoon tea. The ancient poet has no artifice at all. His heroine simply walks forward and explains her own feelings. But she will come at some moment that seems just the right one; she will come to us through a cloud, as it were, of musical emotion from the Chorus, and her words when she speaks will be frankly the language of poetry. They will be none the less sincere or exact for that.

When Phaedra in the Hippolytus has resolved to die rather than show her love, much less attempt to satisfy it, and yet has been so weakened by her long struggle that she will not be able to resist much longer, she explains herself to the Chorus in a long speech:

O Women, dwellers in this portal seat
Of Pelops' land, looking towards my Crete,
How oft, in other days than these, have I
Through night's long hours thought of man's misery
And how this life is wrecked! And, to mine eyes,
Not in man's knowledge, not in wisdom, lies
The lack that makes for sorrow. Nay, we scan
And know the right—for wit hath many a man—
But will not to the last end strive and serve.
For some grow too soon weary, and some swerve
To other paths, setting before the right
The diverse far-off image of Delight,
And many are delights beneath the sun. . . .

It is not the language that any real woman ever spoke, and it is not meant to be. But it is exactly the thought which this woman may have thought and felt, transmuted into a special kind of high poetry. And the women of the Chorus who are listening to it are like no kind of concrete earthly listeners; they are the sort of listeners that are suited to thoughts rather than words, and their own answer at the end comes not like a real comment but like a note of music. When she finishes, defending her resolve to die rather than sin:

O'er all this earth
To every false man that hour comes apace
When Time holds up a mirror to his face,
And marvelling, girl-like, there he stares to see
How foul his heart.—Be it not so with me!

They answer:

Ah, God, how sweet is virtue and how wise,
And honour its due meed in all men's eyes!

"A commonplace?" "A not very original remark?" There is no need for any original remark; what is needed is a note of harmony in words and thought, and that is what we are given.

At a later stage in the play we shall come on another fixed element in the tragedy, the Messenger's Speech. It was probably in the ritual. It was expected in the play. And it was—and is still on the stage—immensely dramatic and effective. Modern writers like Mr. Masefield and Mr. Wilfred Blunt have seen what use can be made of a Messenger's speech. Now for the understanding of the speech itself, what is needed is to read it several times, to mark out exactly the stages of story told, and the gradual rising of emotion and excitement up to the highest point, which is, as usual, near the end but not at the end. The end sinks back to something like calm. It would take too long to analyse a particular Messenger's speech paragraph by paragraph, and the printed page cannot, of course, illustrate the constant varieties of tension, of pace and of emphasis that are needed. But I find the following notes for the guidance of an actor opposite the Messenger's Speech in an old copy of my Hippolytus. Opposite the first lines comes, "Quiet, slow, simple." Then "quicker." "Big" (at "O Zeus . . . hated me.") Then "Drop tension: story." "Pause: more interest." "Mystery." "Awe; rising excitement." "Excitement well controlled." "Steady excitement; steady; swifter." "Up; excitement rising." "Up; but still controlled." "Up;

full steam; let it go." "Highest point." "Down to quiet." "Mystery." "Pause." "End steady: with emotion." These notes have, of course, no authority: as they stand they are due partly to my own conjecture, partly to observation of a remarkable performance. But they have this interest about them. They grow out of the essential nature of the speech and probably would, in their general tenour, be accepted by most students; and further, some very similar scheme would suit not only almost every Messenger's Speech, but also, with the necessary modifications, almost every Greek tragedy as a whole. The quiet beginning, the constant rise of tension through various moods and various changes of tone up to a climax; the carefully arranged drop from the climax to the steady close, without bathos and without any wrecking of the continuity.

But there is another point about Messengers that can be more easily illustrated. Their entrance in Euripides is nearly always carefully prepared. The point is of cardinal importance and needs some explanation. In mere literature it is the words that matter; in dramatic literature it is partly the words, and partly the situation in which they are uttered. A Messenger's Speech ought not only to be a good story in itself, but it ought to be so prepared and led up to that before the speaker begins we are longing to hear what he has to say. An instance of a Messenger's speech with no preparation is in Sophocles' Oedipus, The King (I do not at all suggest that preparation is needed; very likely the situation itself is enough.) Oedipus has rushed into the house in a fury of despair, and the Messenger simply walks out of the house crying

O ye above this land in honour old
Exalted, what a tale shall ye be told,
What sights shall see and tears of horror shed. . . .

Contrast with this the preparation in the Hippolytus (1153 ff.). Hippolytus, cursed, and of course wrongfully cursed, by his father, Theseus, has gone forth to exile. His friends and the women of the Chorus have been grieving for him: Theseus has refused to listen to any plea. Then

LEADER OF THE CHORUS
Look yonder! . . . Surely from the Prince 'tis one
That cometh, full of haste and woe-begone.

We are all watching; a man in great haste enters.
Observe what he says.

HENCHMAN
Ye women, whither shall I go to seek
King Theseus? Is he in this dwelling? Speak!

Our suspense deepens. The **Leader** evidently has hesitated in her answer; she wants to ask a question.... But at this moment the door opens and she falls back:

LEADER
Lo, where he cometh through the Castle Gate.

Through the gate comes **Theseus**, wrapped in gloom, evidently trying still to forget **Hippolytus**. The **Henchman** crosses his path.

HENCHMAN

O King, I bear thee tidings of dire weight
To thee, yea, and to every man, I ween,
From Athens to the marches of Trozên.

Will **Theseus** guess? Will he see that this is one of his son's servants? At any rate he shows no sign of so doing.

THESEUS

What? Some new stroke hath touched, unknown to me
The sister cities of my sovranty?

HENCHMAN

Hippolytus is. . . . Nay, not dead; but stark
Outstretched, a hairsbreadth this side of the dark.

The forbidden name is spoken; there is evidently a moment of shock, but how will **Theseus** take the news? Will he soften?

THESEUS (As though unmoved)

How slain? Was there some other man, whose wife
He had like mine defiled, who sought his life?

Stung by the taunt the **Henchman** answers boldly.

HENCHMAN

His own wild team destroyed him, and the dire
Curse of thy lips. . . . The boon of the great Sire
Is granted thee, O King, and thy son slain.

Will Theseus turn in fury on the speaker?
Or will he even now soften? Neither.

THESEUS

Ye Gods! . . . And thou, Poseidon, not in vain
I called thee Father. Thou hast heard my prayer.

The shock is heavy but he recovers his calm, and with it comes the horrible conviction that his curse was just and the gods have struck dead a guilty man.

How did he die? Speak on. How closed the snare
Of Heaven to slay the shamer of my blood?

Then the **Messenger** begins his story.

Such preparations are regular in Euripides. In the Electra, Orestes has gone forth to find King Aegisthus, and if possible slay him. Electra is waiting in her hut, a drawn sword across her knees, sworn to die if Orestes fails. How is the Messenger brought on? First the Leader of the Chorus thinks she hears a noise in the distance; she is not sure. . . . Yes; a noise of fighting! She calls Electra, who comes, the sword in her hand. The noise increases; a cry; cheering. Something has happened, but what? The cheers sound like Argive voices; "Aegisthus's men!" cries Electra; "then let me die!" The Chorus restrain her. "There is no Messenger; Orestes would have sent a Messenger." "Wait, wait!" cries the Leader, holding her arm: and a man rushes in, shouting, "Victory! Orestes has slain Aegisthus, and we are free" (747-773).

That seems enough, but even now Euripides has not extracted his full effect from the situation. Electra, steeped to the lips in fears and suspicions, recoils from the man. "Who are you? . . . It is a plot!" She must get the sword. . . . The Man bids her look at him again; he is her brother's servant; she saw him with Orestes an hour ago. She looks, remembers, and throws her arms round the man's neck. "Tell me again. Tell me all that happened." And so the **Messenger** begins.

This art of preparation belongs, of course, to the modern stage as much as to the ancient, or more. So do the similar arts of making the right juncture between scenes, of arranging the contrasts and clashes, and especially of so ending each scene as to make the spectator look eagerly for the next move. He must be given just enough notion of the future to whet his appetite; not enough to satisfy it. These are general rules that apply to all good drama. They can all be studied in Mr. Archer's book, Play-Making: A Manual of Craftsmanship. In ancient times they were more developed by Euripides than by his predecessors, but that is all we need say.

Prologue; Set Speech; Messenger; there still remain two stumbling-blocks to a modern reader of Greek tragedies, the Deus ex Mâchinâ, (or "God from the Machine") and the Chorus.

About the appearance of the god we need say little. We have seen above that an epiphany of some Divine Being or a Resurrection of some dead Hero seems to have been an integral part of the old ritual and thus has its natural place in tragedy. His special duty is to bring the action to a quiet close and to ordain the ritual on which the tragedy is based—thus making the performance itself a fulfilment of the god's command (see above p. 66). The actual history of this epiphany is curious. As far as our defective evidence allows us to draw conclusions we can make out that Aeschylus habitually used a divine epiphany, but that he generally kept it for the last play of a trilogy; that he often had a whole galaxy of gods, and that, with some exceptions, his gods walked the floor of earth with the other actors. (The evidence for this is given in Miss Harrison's Themis, pp. 347 ff.) Sophocles, moving towards a more "natural" and less ritual tragedy, used the divine epiphany comparatively little. Euripides, somewhat curiously for one so hostile to the current mythology, intensified this ritual element in drama as he did all the others. And he used it more and more as he grew older. He evidently liked it for its own sake.

There is one view about the Deus ex Mâchinâ which needs a word of correction. It is widely entertained and comes chiefly from Horace's Ars Poetica. It takes the Deus as a device—and a very unskilful one—for somehow finishing a story that has got into a hopeless tangle. The poet is supposed to have piled up ingenious complications and troubles until he cannot see any way out and has to cut the knot by the intervention of something miraculous—in this case, of a machine-made god. Now devices of this sort—the sudden appearance of rich uncles, the discovery of new wills, or of infants changed at birth and the like—are more or less common weaknesses in romantic literature. Hence it was natural that Horace's view about Euripides's god should be uncritically accepted. But as a matter of fact it is a mere mistake. It never in any single case holds good—not even in the Orestes. And there are some plays, like the Iphigenîa in Tauris, in which, so far from the god coming to clear up a tangled plot, the plot has to be diverted at the last moment so as to provide an excuse for the god's arrival. Euripides evidently liked a supernatural ending, and when he had to do without a real god—as in the Medea and the Hecuba—he was apt to end with winged chariots and prophecies. Can we in the least understand what he gained by it?

We must remember one or two things. The epiphany was in the ritual. It was no new invention in itself; the only new thing, apparently, was an improved piece of stage machinery enabling the god to appear more effectively. Further, if we try to put ourselves into the minds of fifth century Greeks, there was probably nothing absurd, nothing even unlikely, in supposing the visible appearance of a god in such an atmosphere as that of tragedy. The heroes and heroines of tragedy were themselves almost divine; they were all figures in the great heroic saga and almost all of them—the evidence is clear—received actual worship. If Orestes or Agamemnon is present on the stage, it is not surprising that Apollo should appear to them. It is, I think, chiefly due to the mistake of over-emphasizing the realism of Euripides that recent writers—myself at one time included—have been so much troubled over these divine epiphanies.

I suspect, also, that we are troubled by a difference of convention about the way in which supernatural beings ought to speak. We moderns like them to be abrupt, thunderous, wrapped in mystery. We expect the style of ancient Hebrew or Norse poetry. Probably a Greek would think both barbaric. At any rate the Greek gods, both in Euripides and elsewhere, affect a specially smooth and fluent and lucid utterance.

And apart from the artistic convention there is a historical consideration which we must never forget, though we are constantly tempted to do so. A well-educated Athenian of the fifth century before Christ was, after all, not as securely lifted above what he called "primaeval simplicity" as a similar man in Western Europe in the eighteenth or nineteenth century after. He was just beginning, with great daring and brilliance, to grasp at something like a philosophic or scientific view of the world; but his hold was very precarious and partial, and when it slipped he fell unsuspectingly into strange abysses. A visible god in the theatre laid probably no more strain on his credulity than, say, a prophetic dream on ours.

However, the above considerations are only pleas in mitigation of sentence. They tend to show that the Deus ex Mâchinâ was not in itself ridiculous to the contemporaries of Euripides; we must go further and try to see why he liked it. The best way is simply, with our antecedent prejudices removed, to read and re-read some of the best epiphany scenes; those, for instance, which close the Electra, the Hippolytus, the Rhesus or the Andromache. We have already seen in the Electra how the poet can use his gods for delivering his essential moral judgment on the story; the condemnation of revenge, the pity for mankind, the opening up of a larger atmosphere in which the horror through which we have just passed falls into its due resting-place. In the Hippolytus the sheer beauty of the Artemis scene speaks for itself and makes a marvellous ending. Notably it attains an effect which could scarcely be reached in any other way, a strange poignant note amid the beauty, where mortal emotion breaks against the cliffs of immortal calm. After many words of tenderness Artemis finishes (1437 ff.):

Farewell! I may not watch man's fleeting breath,
Nor stain mine eyes with the effluence of death.
And sure that terror now is very near. . . .
(The Goddess slowly rises and floats away.)

HIPPOLYTUS
Farewell! Farewell, most blessed! Lift thee clear
Of soiling men. Thou wilt not grieve in heaven
For our long love. . . . Father, thou art forgiven;

It was Her will; I am not wroth with thee. . . .
I have obeyed her all my days!

Of course the epiphany does not give what our jaded senses secretly demand, a strong "curtain." It gives the antique peaceful close. The concrete men and women whom we have seen before us, striving and suffering, dissolve into the beautiful mist of legend; strife and passion and sharp cries sink away into the telling of old fables; then the fables themselves have their lines of consequence reaching out to touch the present world and the thing that we are doing now; to make it the fulfilment of an ancient command or prophecy, to give it a meaning that we had never realized; and thus we are awakened to the concrete theatre and the audience and the life about us not with a shock but gradually, like one lying with his eyes half shut and thinking about a dream that has just gone.

I do not for a moment say that the divine epiphany is the right, or even the best, way of ending any tragedy; I only plead that if we use our imaginations we can find in it a very rare beauty and can understand why one of the greatest of the world's dramatists held to it so firmly.

CHAPTER IX

THE ART OF EURIPIDES CONTINUED: THE CHORUS: CONCLUSION

And lastly there is the Chorus, at once the strangest and the most beautiful of all these ancient and remote conventions. If we can understand the Chorus we have got to the very heart of Greek tragedy.

The objections to the Chorus are plain to any infant. These dozen homogeneous persons, old men or young women, eternally present and almost never doing anything, intruded on action that often demands the utmost privacy: their absurdity, on any plane of realism, is manifest. We need waste no more words upon it. Verisimilitude is simply thrown to the winds. That is, no doubt, a great sacrifice, and fine artists do not as a rule incur a sacrifice without making sure of some compensating gain. Let us try to find out what that gain was, or at least what the great Greek artists were aiming at. And let us begin by forgetting the modern stage altogether and thinking ourselves back to the very origins of drama.

The word "chorus" means "dance" or "dancing-ground." There were such dancing floors on Greek soil before ever the Greeks came there. They have been found in prehistoric Crete and in the islands. We hear in Homer of the "houses and dancing-grounds" of the Morning Star. The dance was as old as mankind; only it was a kind of dance that we have almost forgotten. The ancient dance was not, like our ballets, rooted in sexual emotion. It was religious: it was a form of prayer. It consisted in the use of the whole body, every limb and every muscle, to express somehow that overflow of emotion for which a man has no words. And primitive man had less command of words than we have. When the men were away on the war-path, the women prayed for them with all their bodies. They danced for the men's safe return. When the tribe's land was parching for lack of rain the tribesmen danced for the rain to come. The dance did not necessarily imply movement. It might consist in simply maintaining the same rigid attitude, as when Moses held out his arms during the battle with the Amalekites or Ahure in the Egyptian story waited kneeling and fasting for Nefrekepta's return.

Now if we consider what kind of emotion will specially call for this form of expression it is easy to see that it will be the sort that tends quickly to get beyond words: religious emotions of all kinds, helpless desire, ineffectual regret and all feelings about the past. When we think of the kind of ritual from which tragedy emerged, the lament for a dead god, we can see how well a dance was fitted, in primitive times, to express the emotions that we call tragic.

This dance gradually grew into drama; how it did so is an old story. Into the inarticulate mass of emotion and dumb show which is the Dance there comes some more articulate element. There comes some one who relates, or definitely enacts, the actual death or "pathos" of the hero, while the Chorus goes on as before expressing emotion about it. This emotion, it is easy to see, may be quite different from that felt by the Hero. There is implied in the contemplation of any great deed this ultimate emotion, which is not as a rule felt by the actual doers of it, and is not, at its highest power, to be expressed by the ordinary language of dialogue. The dramatist may make his characters express all that they can properly feel; he may put into articulate dialogue all that it will bear. But there still remains some residue which no one on the stage can personally feel and which can only express itself as music or yearning of the body. This residue finds its one instrument in the Chorus.

Imagine the death of some modern hero, of Lincoln or of Nelson, treated in the Greek form. We should have first a Messenger bringing news of the battle of Trafalgar or the pistol-shot in the Washington Theatre. The hero would be borne in dying; his friends would weep over him; we should hear his last words. But there would always remain some essential emotion or reflection—sadness, triumph, pathos, thoughts of the future from which this man will be lacking or of the meaning of this death in human history: neither Lincoln nor Nelson can express this, nor without falsity any of their human companions. In a novel the author can express it; in a modern play or a severely realistic novel it is generally not expressed except by a significant silence or some symbol. For realistic work demands extreme quickness in its audience, and can only make its effect on imaginations already trained by romance and idealism. On the Greek stage the Chorus will be there just for this purpose, to express in music and movement this ultimate emotion and, as Mr. Haigh puts it, to "shed a lyrical splendour over the whole." It will translate the particular act into something universal. It will make a change in all that it touches, increasing the elements of beauty and significance and leaving out or reducing the element of crude pain. This is nothing extraordinary: it is the normal business of poetry, at least of great tragic poetry. An actual bereavement is an experience consisting of almost nothing but crude pain; when it is translated into religion or poetry, into "Rachel weeping for her children," or into "Break, break, break," it has somehow become a thing of beauty and even of comfort.

The important thing to observe is what Mr. F. M. Cornford has explained in his Thucydides Mythistoricus (pp. 144 ff.), that a Greek tragedy normally proceeds in two planes or two worlds. When the actors are on the stage we are following the deeds and fates of so many particular individuals, lovers, plotters, enemies, or whatever they are, at a particular point of time and space. When the stage is empty and the Choral Odes begin, we have no longer the particular acts and places and persons but something universal and eternal. The body, as it were, is gone and the essence remains. We have the greatness of love, the vanity of revenge, the law of eternal retribution, or perhaps the eternal doubt whether in any sense the world is governed by righteousness.

Thus the talk about improbability with which we started falls into its proper insignificance. The Chorus in Euripides is frequently blamed by modern scholars on the ground that "it does not further the action," that its presence is "improbable," or its odes "irrelevant." The answer is that none of these things constitute the business of the Chorus; its business is something considerably higher and more important.

Of action and relevancy we will speak later. They are both closely connected with the question of verisimilitude. And as for verisimilitude, we simply do not think of it. We are not imitating the outside of life. We are expressing its soul, not depicting its body. And if we did attempt verisimilitude we should find that in a Chorus it is simply unattainable. In Nelson's case a Chorus of Sailors would be every bit as improbable as a Chorus of Mermaids or Angels, and on the whole rather more strikingly so. If we try to think of the most effective Choruses in modern tragedies, I do not think we shall hit on any bands of Strolling Players or Flower Girls or Church Choirs or other Choruses that aim at "naturalness"; we shall probably go straight to the Choruses of Spirits in Prometheus Unbound or those of The Ages and The Pities in Mr. Hardy's Dynasts. The Chorus belongs not to the plane of ordinary experience, where people are real and act and make apposite remarks, but to that higher world where in Mr. Cornford's words "metaphor, as we call it, is the very stuff of life."

With very few exceptions, Greek Choruses are composed of beings who are naturally the denizens or near neighbours of such a world. Sometimes they are frankly supernatural, as in the Eumenides, or half supernatural, as in the Bacchae; sometimes they are human beings seen through the mist of a great emotion, like the weeping Rachels of the Suppliant Women; the captives of the Trojan Women or the Iphigenîa; the old men who dream dreams in the Heracles. Even if they start as common men or women, sooner or later they become transformed.

The problem of the Chorus to Euripides was not how to make it as little objectionable as possible; it was how to get the greatest and highest value out of it. And that resolves itself largely into the problem of handling these two planes of action, using now the lower and now the upper, now keeping them separate, now mingling them, and at times letting one forcibly invade the other. I cannot here go into details of the various effects obtained from the Chorus by Euripides; but I will take a few typical ones, selecting in each case scenes that have been loudly condemned by critics.

The first and most normal effect is to use the Chorus for "relief"; to bring in, as it were, the ideal world to heal the wounds of the real. It is not, of course, "comic relief," as indulged in so freely by the Elizabethans. It is a transition from horror or pain to mere beauty or music, with hardly any change of tension. I mean, that if the pain has brought tears to your eyes, the beauty will be such as to keep them there, while of course changing their character. It is this use of lyrics that enables the Greek playwright to treat freely scenes of horror and yet never lose the prevailing atmosphere of high beauty. Look at the Salamis Chorus in the Trojan Women immediately following the child's death; the lyrics between Oedipus and the Chorus when he has just entered with his bleeding eyes; or, in particular, the song sung by the Chorus in Hippolytus just after Phaedra has rushed off to kill herself. We have had a scene of high tension and almost intolerable pain, and the Chorus, left alone, make certainly no relevant remarks. I can think of no relevant remark that would not be an absurd bathos. They simply break out (732 ff.):

Could I take me to some cavern for mine hiding,
In the hill-tops, where the sun scarce hath trod,
Or a cloud make the home of mine abiding,
As a bird among the bird-droves of God. . . .

It is just the emotion that was in our own hearts; the cry for escape to some place, however sad, that is still beautiful: to the poplar grove by the Adriatic where his sisters weep for Phaethon; or, at last, as the song continues and grows bolder, to some place that has happiness as well as beauty; to that "strand of the Daughters of the Sunset,"

Where a sound of living waters never ceaseth
In God's quiet garden by the sea,
And Earth, the ancient Life-giver, increaseth
Joy among the meadows, like a tree.

And the wish for escape brings an actual escape, on some wind of beauty, as it were, from the Chorus's own world. This is, on the whole, the most normal use of the Choric odes, though occasionally they may also be used for helping on the action. For instance, in the ode immediately following that just quoted the Chorus gives a sort of prophetic or clairvoyant description of Phaedra's suicide.

But the Greek Chorus does not only sing its great odes on an empty stage; it also carries on, by the mouth of its Leader, a certain amount of ordinary dialogue with the actors. Its work here is generally kept unobtrusive, neutral and low-toned. When a traveller wants to ask his way; when the hero or heroine announces some resolve, or gives some direction, the Leader is there to make the necessary response. But only within certain carefully guarded limits. The Leader must never become a definite full-blooded character with strongly personal views. He must never take really effective or violent action. He never, I think, gives information which we do not already possess or expresses views which could seem paradoxical or original. He is an echo, a sort of music in the air. This comes out clearly in another fine scene of the Hippolytus, where Phaedra is listening at the door and the Leader of the Chorus listens with her, echoing and making more vibrant Phaedra's own emotion (565-600).

At times, in these dialogue scenes, an effect is obtained by allowing the Chorus to turn for a moment into ordinary flesh and blood. In the Iphigenía in Tauris (1055 ff.) the safe escape of Iphigenía and Orestes depends on the secrecy of the Chorus of Greek captives. Iphigenía implores them to be silent, and, after a moment of hesitation, because of the danger, they consent. Iphigenía, with one word of radiant gratitude, forgets all about them and leaves the stage to arrange things with her brother. And the captives left alone watch a sea-bird winging its way towards Argos, whither Iphigenía is now going and they shall never go, and break into a beautiful home-sick song. Similarly in the splendid finale of Aeschylus' Prometheus the Daughters of Ocean, who have been mostly on the unearthly plane throughout the play, are suddenly warned to stand aside and leave Prometheus before his doom falls: in a rush of human passion they refuse to desert him and are hurled with him into Hell.

At other times the effect is reached by emphasizing just the other side, the unearthliness of the Chorus. In the Heracles, for instance, when the tyrant Lycus is about to make some suppliants leave the protection of an altar by burning them—a kind of atrocity which just avoided the technical religious offence of violating sanctuary—the Chorus of old men tries for a moment to raise its hand against the tyrant's soldiers. It is like the figures of a dream trying to fight—"words and a hidden-featured thing seen in a dream of the night," as the poet himself says, trying to battle against flesh and blood; a helpless visionary transient struggle which is beautiful for a moment but would be grotesque if it lasted. Again, in the lost Antiope there is a scene where the tyrant is inveigled into a hut by murderers; he manages to dash out and appeals to the Chorus of old men for help. But they are not really old men; they are only ancient echoes or voices of Justice, who speak his doom upon him, standing moveless while the slayers come.

These examples enable us to understand a still stronger effect of the same kind which occurs in the Medea and has, until very lately, been utterly condemned and misunderstood. It is an effect rather reminding one of the Greek fable of a human wrong so terrible that it shook the very Sun out of his course. It is like the human cry in the Electra (p. 157), which shook the eternal peace of the gods in heaven. There is something delirious about it, an impossible invasion of the higher world by the lower, a shattering of unapproachable bars.

Medea has gone to murder her children inside the house. The Chorus is left chanting its own, and our, anguish outside. "Why do they not rush in and save the children?" asked the critics. In the first place, because that is not the kind of action that a Chorus can ever perform. That needs flesh and blood. "Well," the critic continues, "if they cannot act effectively, why does Euripides put them in a position in which we instinctively clamour for effective action and they are absurd if they do not act?" The answer to that is given in the play itself. They do not rush in; there is no question of their rushing in: because the door is barred. When Jason in the next scene tries to enter the house he has to use soldiers with crowbars. The only action they can possibly perform is the sort that specially belongs to the Chorus, the action of baffled desire.

Medea is in the house; the Chorus is chanting its sublimated impersonal emotion about the Love that has turned to Hate in Medea, and its dread of things to come (1267 ff.):

For fierce are the smitings back of blood once shed
Where Love hath been: God's wrath upon them that kill,
And an anguished Earth, and the wonder of the dead
Haunting as music still. . . .

when a sudden cry is heard within. The song breaks short, and one woman speaks:

Hark! Did ye hear? Heard ye the children's cry?

Another
O miserable woman! O abhorred!

Voice of a Child within
What shall I do? What is it? Keep me fast
From Mother!

The Other Child
I know nothing. Brother! Oh,
I think she means to kill us.

One of the Chorus
Let me go!
I will!—Help, help! And save them at the last!

Child
Yes, in God's name. Help quickly or we die!

The Other Child
She has almost caught me now: she has a sword.

One sees the Women of the Chorus listening for the Children's words; then they break, as it were, from the spell of their own super-mortal atmosphere, and fling themselves on the barred door. They beat in vain against the bars and the Children's voices cry for help from the other side.

But the inrush of violent horror is only tolerated for a moment. Even in the next words we are moving back to the realm of formal poetry:

Women (Beating at the Door)
Thou stone, thou thing of iron! Wilt verily
Spill with thine hand that life, the vintage stored
Of thine own agony?

Others
A woman slew her babes in days of yore,
One, only one, from dawn to eventide. . . .

and in a moment we are away in a beautiful remote song about far-off children who have been slain in legend. That death-cry is no longer a shriek heard in the next room. It is the echo of many cries of children from the beginning of the world, children who are now at peace and whose ancient pain has become part mystery and part music. Memory—that Memory who was mother of the Muses—has done her work upon it.

We see here the justification of the high formalism and convention of Greek tragedy. It can touch without flinching any horror of tragic life, without failing in sincerity and without marring its normal atmosphere of beauty. It brings things under the great magic of something which is hard to name, but which I have tried in these pages to indicate; something that we can think of as eternity or the universal or perhaps even as Memory. For Memory, used in this way, has a magical power. As Mr. Bertrand Russell has finely put it in one of his Essays, "The Past does not change or strive. Like Duncan in Macbeth 'After life's fitful fever it sleeps well.' What was eager and grasping, what was petty and transitory, has faded away. The things that were beautiful and eternal shine out like stars in the night."

This power of transfiguration belongs in varying degrees to all poetry, but it belongs in special force to Greek Tragedy; and Greek Tragedy attains it in part by all its high religious traditions and severities of form, but most fully by means of its strangest convention, the Chorus; the band of half-embodied emotions and memories, the lyric song and the dance expressing things beyond speech. It is through this power that tragedy attain its peculiar quality of encouragement and triumph. We must not forget that Aristotle, a judge whose dicta should seldom be dismissed without careful reflection, distinguishes tragedy from other forms of drama not as the form that represents human misery but as that which represents human goodness or nobleness. If his MSS. are to be trusted he even goes so far as to say that tragedy is "the representation of Eudaimonia," or the higher kind of happiness. Of course he fully recognizes the place of death and disaster in it, and he prefers the so-called "unhappy ending." The powers of evil and horror must be granted their full scope; it is only thus that we can triumph over them. Only when they have worked their uttermost will do we realize that there remains something in man's soul which is forever beyond their grasp and has power in its own right to make life beautiful. That is the great revelation, or the great illusion, of tragedy.

It is achieved, apparently, by a combination of two extremes; in matter a full facing of tragic facts, and in form a resolute transfiguration of them by poetry. The weak artist shirks the truth by a feeble idealism;

the prosaic artist fails to transfigure it. Euripides seems to me to have gone further than any other writer in the attempt to combine in one unity these separate poles. In this lies, for good or evil, his unique quality as a poet. To many readers it seems that his powers failed him; his mixture of real life and supernatural atmosphere, of wakeful thought and dreaming legend, remains a discord, a mere jar of overwrought conventions and violent realism. To others it is because of this very quality that he has earned the tremendous rank accorded him by Goethe, and in a more limited sense by Aristotle, and still stands out, as he stood over two thousand years ago, "even if faulty in various ways, at any rate clearly the most tragic of the poets."

PRONUNCIATION OF GREEK NAMES

Greek names have mostly come to the modern world through Latin and consequently are generally given in their Latin form. Thus in Latin the K-sound was denoted by C; KH by CH, AI- by AE; OU- by U; U by Y, which is really a Greek letter taken over into Latin for this express purpose. Also one or two common terminations are given in their Latin form, Homêros becoming Homerus, Apollon Apollo, and Alexandros Alexander. This difference in writing did not mean a difference in pronunciation; the Latin Aeschylus was pronounced (except perhaps in the termination) exactly like the Greek "Aiskhulos," Thucydides like "Thoukudides."

The conventional English pronunciation follows the Latin form and pronounces all vowels and diphthongs as in English, except that E is always pronounced, and never used merely to lengthen a previous vowel: e.g., "Euripides" rhymes with "insipid ease," not with "glides," "Hermione" roughly with "bryony," not with "tone." OE and AE are pronounced as one syllable, like "ee" in "free," except when marked as two syllables, as "Arsinoë." EU as in "feud." Of the consonants C is pronounced as in English, CH as K. The only difficulty then is to know where the stress comes and what vowels are long or short.

By Latin custom, if the last syllable but one is long, it will have the stress (as surprísing, everlásting, Achílles, Agamémnon); if the last syllable but one is short, the stress will be on the syllable before (as ádamant, dángerous, Aéschylus, Thucýdides).

In the following index ´ denotes a stressed short vowel sound, as in cáttle, imbédded, pítiful, bíology: ^ denotes a stressed long vowel as in câke, creêper, spîteful, Octôber, endûrable, g[^y]roscope. In the case of the letter "y", this length has been indicated by [^y].

Euripides – A Short Biography

Euripides is rightly lauded as one of the great dramatists of all time. In his lifetime, he wrote over 90 plays and although only 18 have survived they reveal the scope and reach of his genius.

Euripides is identified with many theatrical innovations that have influenced drama all the way down to modern times, especially in the representation of traditional, mythical heroes as ordinary people in extraordinary circumstances. This new approach led him to pioneer developments that later writers would adapt to comedy. Yet he also became "the most tragic of poets", focusing on the inner lives and motives of his characters in a way previously unknown. He was "the creator of...that cage which is the theatre of Shakespeare's Othello, Racine's Phèdre, of Ibsen and Strindberg," in which "...imprisoned men and women destroy each other by the intensity of their loves and hates", and yet he was also the literary ancestor of comic dramatists as diverse as Menander and George Bernard Shaw.

As would be expected from a life lived 2,500 years ago, details of it are few and far between. Accounts of his life, written down the ages, do exist but whether much is reliable or surmised is open to debate.

Most accounts agree that he was born on Salamis Island around 480 BC, to mother Cleito and father Mnesarchus, a retailer who lived in a village near Athens. Upon the receipt of an oracle saying that his son was fated to win "crowns of victory", Mnesarchus insisted that the boy should train for a career in athletics.

His education was not only confined to athletics: he also studied painting and philosophy under the masters Prodicus and Anaxagoras.

However, what became quickly very clear was that athletics was not to be his way to win crowns of victory. Euripides had been lucky enough to have been born in the era as the other two masters of Greek Tragedy; Sophocles and Æschylus. It was in their footsteps that he was destined to follow.

His first play was performed some thirteen years after the first of Socrates plays and a mere three years after Æschylus had written his classic The Oristria.

Theatre was becoming a very important part of the Greek culture. The Dionysia, held annually, was the most important festival of theatre and second only to the fore-runner of the Olympic games, the Panathenia, held every four years, in its appeal. It was a large festival in ancient Athens in honor of the god Dionysus, the central events of which were the theatrical performances of dramatic tragedies and, from 487 BC, comedies. The Dionysia actually consisted of two related festivals, the Rural Dionysia and the City Dionysia, which took place in different parts of the year.

Euripides first competed in the City Dionysia, in 455 BC, one year after the death of Æschylus, and, incredibly, it was not until 441 BC that he won first prize. His final competition in Athens was in 408 BC. However, The Bacchae and Iphigenia in Aulis were performed after his death in 405 BC and first prize was awarded posthumously. Altogether his plays won first prize only five times.

His plays, and those of Æschylus and Sophocles, indicate a difference in outlook between the three men, most easily explained as a generational gap, although with three great talents overlapping the driving forces may have pushed individual styles onwards perhaps faster than they may otherwise have done. Æschylus still looked back to the archaic period, Sophocles was in transition between periods, and Euripides was fully bonded with the new spirit of the classical age. When Euripides' plays are sequenced in time, they also show a developing pattern:

An early period of high tragedy (Medea, Hippolytus)
A patriotic period at the outset of the Peloponnesian War (Children of Hercules, Suppliants)
A middle period of disillusionment at the senselessness of war (Hecuba, Women of Troy)
An escapist period with a focus on romantic intrigue (Ion, Iphigenia in Tauris, Helen)
A final period of tragic despair (Orestes, Phoenician Women, Bacchae)

However, with over three quarters of his plays lost it is difficult to be certain as to whether the other works would also represent this development (e.g., Iphigenia at Aulis is dated with the 'despairing' Bacchae, yet it contains elements that became typical of New Comedy). In the Bacchae, he restores the chorus and messenger speech to their traditional role in the tragic plot, and the play appears to be the culmination of a regressive or archaizing tendency in his later works.

In one of his earliest surviving plays, Medea, includes a speech that he seems to have written in defence of himself as an intellectual ahead of his time, and to further challenge the times he has put the words in the mouth of the play's heroine:

"If you introduce new, intelligent ideas to fools, you will be thought frivolous, not intelligent. On the other hand, if you do get a reputation for surpassing those who are supposed to be intellectually sophisticated, you will seem to be a thorn in the city's flesh. This is what has happened to me."—Medea.

As we know Athenian tragedies during Euripides' lifetime were a public contest between playwrights. The state funded that contest and awarded prizes to the winners. The language was spoken and sung verse, the performance area included a circular floor or orchestra where the chorus could dance, a space for actors (usually three speaking actors in Euripides' time), a backdrop or skene and some special effects: an ekkyklema (used to bring the skene's "indoors" outdoors) and a mechane (used to lift actors in the air, as in deus ex machina). With the introduction of the third actor (an innovation attributed to Sophocles), acting also began to be regarded as a skill to be rewarded with prizes, requiring a long apprenticeship in the chorus. Euripides and other playwrights accordingly composed more and more arias for accomplished actors to sing and this tendency becomes more marked in his later plays: tragedy for him was a living and ever-changing genre.

Accounts by the famed comic poet, Aristophanes, characterise Euripides as a spokesman for destructive, new ideas, that mirror or help to bring about declining standards in both society and tragedy. However, 5th century tragedy was a social gathering for "carrying out quite publicly the maintenance and development of mental infrastructure" and it offered spectators a "platform for an utterly unique form of institutionalized discussion". A dramatist's role was not just to entertain but also to educate his fellow citizens—he was expected to have a message. Clearly this use of drama to democratize discussion was a very useful tool for all sides. Traditional myth provided the subject matter but the dramatist was meant to be innovative so as to sustain interest, which led to novel characterization of heroic figures and to use the mythical past to talk about present issues. The difference between Euripides and his older colleagues was, again, one of degree: his characters talked about the present more controversially and more pointedly than did those of Æschylus and Sophocles, sometimes even challenging the democratic order. Thus, for example, Odysseus is represented in Hecuba as "agile-minded, sweet-talking, demos-pleasing" i.e., a type of the war-time demagogues that were active in Athens during the Peloponnesian War. His concept is pleasingly simple. He retains the old stories and myths as well as the great names of the past and places them in the lives of contemporary Athenians thereby immediately help the audience understand it from the point of view of their own lives.

As mouthpieces for contemporary issues, they all seem to have had at least an elementary course in public speaking. Sometimes the dialogue often contrasts so strongly with the mythical and heroic setting, it looks as if Euripides aimed at parody, as for example in The Trojan Women, where the heroine's rationalized prayer provokes comment from Menelaus:

Hecuba:...O Zeus, whether you are the Law of Necessity in nature, or the Law of Reason in man, hear my prayers. You are everywhere, pursuing your noiseless path, ordering the affairs of mortals according to justice.

Menelaus: What's this? You are starting a new fashion in prayer.

Athenian citizens were familiar with rhetoric in the assembly and law courts, and some scholars believe that Euripides was more interested in his characters as speakers with cases to argue than as characters with lifelike personalities. They are self-conscious about speaking formally and their rhetoric is shown to be flawed, as if Euripides was exploring the problematical nature of language and communication: "For speech points in three different directions at once, to the speaker, to the person addressed, to the features in the world it describes, and each of these directions can be felt as skewed". Thus in the example above, Hecuba presents herself as a sophisticated intellectual describing a rationalised cosmos yet the speech is ill-matched to her audience, Menelaus (an unsophisticated listener), and soon it is found not to suit the cosmos either (her infant grandson is brutally murdered by the victorious Greeks).

Æschylus and Sophocles were innovative, but Euripides could move easily between tragic, comic, romantic and political effects, a versatility that appears in individual plays and also over the course of his career. Potential for comedy lay in his use of 'contemporary' characters, in his sophisticated tone, his relatively informal Greek, and his ingenious use of plots centered on motifs that later became standard, such as the 'recognition scene'. Other tragedians also used recognition scenes but they were heroic in emphasis, as in Æschylus's The Libation Bearers, which Euripides parodied with his mundane treatment of it in Electra (Euripides was unique among the tragedians in incorporating theatrical criticism in his plays). Traditional myth, with its exotic settings, heroic adventures and epic battles, offered potential for romantic melodrama as well as for political comments on a war theme, so that his plays are an extraordinary mix of elements. The Trojan Women for example is a powerfully disturbing play on the theme of war's horrors, apparently critical of Athenian imperialism (it was composed in the aftermath of the Melian massacre and during the preparations for the Sicilian Expedition) yet it features the comic exchange between Menelaus and Hecuba quoted above and the chorus considers Athens, the "blessed land of Theus", to be a desirable refuge—such complexity and ambiguity are typical both of his "patriotic" and "anti-war" plays.

Tragic poets in the 5th century competed against one another at the City Dionysia, each with a tetralogy consisting of three tragedies and a satyr-play. The few extant fragments of satyr-plays attributed to Æschylus and Sophocles indicate that these were a loosely structured, simple and jovial form of entertainment. However, in Cyclops (the only complete Euripides satyr-play that survives) the entertainment is structured more like a tragedy and introduced a note of critical irony typical of his other work. His genre-bending inventiveness is shown above all in Alcestis, a blend of tragic and satyric elements. This fourth play in his tetralogy for 438 BC (i.e., it occupied the position conventionally reserved for satyr-plays) is a "tragedy" that features Heracles as a satyric hero in conventional satyr-play scenes, involving an arrival, a banquet, a victory over an ogre (in this case, Death), a happy ending, a feast and a departure to new adventures.

Euripides was also a great lyric poet. In Medea, for example, he composed for his city, Athens, "the noblest of her songs of praise". His lyric skills however are not just confined to individual poems: "A play of Euripides is a musical whole....one song echoes motifs from the preceding song, while introducing new ones."

Much of his life and his whole career coincided with the struggle between Athens and Sparta for hegemony in Greece but he didn't live to see the final defeat of his city.

It is said that he died in Macedonia after being attacked by the Molossian hounds of King Archelaus and that his cenotaph near Piraeus was struck by lightning—signs of his unique powers, whether for good or ill. In an account by Plutarch, the complete failure of the Sicilian expedition led Athenians to trade renditions of Euripides' lyrics to their enemies in return for food and drink (Life of Nicias 29). Plutarch is the source also for the story that the victorious Spartan generals, having planned the demolition of Athens and the enslavement of its people, grew merciful after being entertained at a banquet by lyrics from Euripides' play Electra: "they felt that it would be a barbarous act to annihilate a city which produced such men" (Life of Lysander).

In The Frogs, composed after Euripides and Æschylus were both dead, Aristophanes imagines the god Dionysus venturing down to Hades in search of a good poet to bring back to Athens. After a debate between the two deceased bards, the god brings Æschylus back to life as more useful to Athens on account of his wisdom, rejecting Euripides as merely clever. Such comic 'evidence' suggests that Athenians admired Euripides even while they mistrusted his intellectualism, at least during the long war with Sparta.

Euripides had a famous library—one of the first to be privately collected. Although he lived most of his life in the midst of the cultured society of Athens, and was in some respects a leader in it, he grew bitter and despondent over the fierce rivalries and greedy ambitions which ran through the city. He loved the seclusion of his house at Salamis, where it was said that he composed his dramas in a cave.

Euripides fell out of favour with his fellow Athenian citizens and retired to the court of Archelaus, king of Macedon, who treated him with consideration and affection.

At his death, in around 406BC, he was mourned by the king, who, refusing the request of the Athenians that his remains be carried back to the Greek city, buried him with much splendor within his own dominions. His tomb was placed at the confluence of two streams, near Arethusa in Macedonia, and a cenotaph was built to his memory on the road from Athens towards the Piraeus.

Euripides – A Concise Bibliography

Alcestis (438 BC)
Medea (431 BC)
Heracleidae (c. 430 BC)
Hippolytus (428 BC)
Andromache (c. 425 BC)
Hecuba (c. 424 BC)
The Suppliants (c. 423 BC)
Electra (c. 420 BC)
Heracles (c. 416 BC)
The Trojan Women (c. 415 BC)
Iphigenia in Tauris (c. 414 BC)
Ion (c. 414 BC)

Helen (c. 412 BC)
Phoenician Women (c. 410 BC)
Orestes (c.408 BC)
Bacchae (405 BC)
Iphigenia at Aulis (405 BC)
Rhesus
Cyclops

Lost and Fragmentary Plays (Dated)

Peliades (455 BC)
Telephus (438 BC with Alcestis)
Alcmaeon in Psophis (438 BC with Alcestis)
Cretan Women (438 with Alcestis)
Cretans (c. 435 BC)
Philoctetes (431 BC with Medea)
Dictys (431 BC with Medea)
Theristai (satyr play, 431 BC with Medea)
Stheneboea (before 429 BC)
Bellerophon (c. 430 BC)
Cresphontes (ca. 425 BC)
Erechtheus (422 BC)
Phaethon (c. 420 BC)
Wise Melanippe (c. 420 BC)
Alexandros (415 BC with Trojan Women)
Palamedes (415 BC with Trojan Women)
Sisyphus (satyr play, 415 BC with Trojan Women)
Captive Melanippe (c. 412 BC)
Andromeda (412 BC with Helen)
Antiope (c. 410 BC)
Archelaus (c. 410 BC)
Hypsipyle (c. 410 BC)
Alcmaeon in Corinth (c. 405 BC) Won first prize as part of a trilogy with The Bacchae and Iphigenia in Aulis.

Lost and Fragmentary Plays (Not Dated)

Aegeus
Aeolus
Alcmene
Alope, or Cercyon
Antigone
Auge
Autolycus
Busiris
Cadmus

Chrysippus
Danae
Epeius
Eurystheus
Hippolytus Veiled
Ino
Ixion
Lamia
Licymnius
Meleager
Mysians
Oedipus
Oeneus
Oenomaus
Peirithous
Peleus
Phoenix
Phrixus
Pleisthenes
Polyidus
Protesilaus
Reapers
Rhadamanthys
Sciron
Scyrians
Syleus
Temenidae
Temenos
Tennes
Theseus
Thyestes